WASTE

UNTIMELY MEDITATIONS

WASTE

A NEW MEDIA PRIMER

ROBERTO SIMANOWSKI

THE MIT PRESS
CAMBRIDGE, MASSACHUSETTS
LONDON, ENGLAND

TRANSLATED BY AMANDA DEMARCO AND SUSAN H. GILLESPIE

This translation © 2018 Massachusetts Institute of Technology

First published as *Abfall: Das alternative ABC der neuen Medien* in the series *Frohliche Wissenschaft* by Matthes & Seitz Berlin: © Matthes & Seitz Berlin Verlagsgesellschaft mbH, Berlin 2017.

This book was set in PF DinText Pro by by Toppan Best-set Premedia Limited. Printed and bound in the United States of America.

Library of Congress Cataloging-in-Publication Data is available.

ISBN: 978-0-262-53627-1

10 9 8 7 6 5 4 3 2 1

CONTENTS

ACKNOWLEDGMENTS

This book draws considerable inspiration from Andreas Huyssen's reflections on the stylistic form of the miniature, *Miniature Metropolis: Literature in an Age of Photography and Film* (2015), as well as his writings on postmodern philosophy and cultural techniques of remembering.

WASTE: AN INTRODUCTION

The development of the "new media"—media that produce digital data, save it, present it, and transfer it; that is, the "Internet" everyone was talking about in the late 1990s— can be characterized in terms of waste and by-products, dissent and decline.[1] The first way to interpret the title of this book is the Internet as a by-product of ARPANET (Advanced Research Projects Agency Network), and ARPANET of MILNET (Military Network). As is so often the case in the history of media, the new is nothing but a by-product of military development.

It began on October 4, 1957, when the Soviet Union shot *Sputnik* into space, demonstrating its technological progress to its potential military opponent the United States. On January 7, 1958, the Pentagon reacted with the founding of DARPA (Defense Advanced Research Projects Agency), an agency for the advancement of military research. To increase the capacities of the participating institutes, in 1969, DARPA connected the mainframe computers of four universities (the Stanford Research Institute; the University of Utah; the University of California, Los Angeles; and the University of California, Santa Barbara) to form the Advanced Research Projects Agency Network. More universities joined in to support the Defense Department's research, so that by 1983, around five hundred computers were connected to each other via ARPANET.

Civilian use of this war technology began unofficially when people began to use the mailing lists (which had been created for ARPANET as a central means of communication) to talk more about sci-fi films than military research. That's why the Pentagon separated the secret MILNET from ARPANET in 1983, leaving the latter for public use, which at first was limited to providing all university faculty with email access. When the National Science Foundation made what was by then called the Internet accessible to the public in 1990, online services such as AOL, Yahoo, Amazon, and eBay began to commercialize it. The key technical terms of this development included Telnet, Usenet, FTP (file transfer protocol), TCP (transmission control protocol), and WWW (World Wide Web), which linked the documents of the Internet in a user-friendly way with hypertext technology starting in 1991, as well as Mosaic, the web browser that allowed graphics and interactive elements to be incorporated into websites beginning in 1993.

The rest is history. Since then, the by-product that is the Internet has influenced all areas of individual and social life. Communication, knowledge acquisition, identity formation, friendships, shopping, watching television, listening to music, planning a vacation, going on vacation, sharing the photos we take on vacation ... nothing is the way it used to be. On January 24, 2013, the consequences of 1957's *Sputnik* shock were established as a new legally protected right: according to a decision by the German Federal

Court, the Internet "has become a medium that decisively influences the lives of a majority of the population, and whose absence is strongly felt in everyday life," meaning that those who deprive someone of it can be held liable for damages.[2]

It could only have come to this because effective waste management was arranged very early on. Under the martial name "SpamAssassin," a filter program "got rid of" spam and junk mail, which had quickly become a central component of communicative noise after the popularization of email and the Internet. Reliable algorithms were necessary to keep communication in the new medium at least somewhat manageable. SpamAssassin and its predecessor filter. plx had been seeing to that since 1997. But that was just the beginning of the management. The future of SpamAssassin also includes "getting rid of" humanity, because garbage disposal in the realm of communications is the first exercise for artificial intelligence.

The software learns to recognize patterns based only on spam, until it is finally able to sort the good emails into your inbox and the bad ones into the trash. All current and future algorithmic analysis and regulation, all of the fantasies of intelligent refrigerators, self-driving cars, and learning robots that fascinate or frighten us today have their beginnings here. SpamAssassin's more dangerous little brother is called the death algorithm, which will decide in cases of emergency if a vehicle should crash into a group of pedestrians, a mother and child, or the wall of a building. This makes moral philosophy a central factor of automotive production, because in the future our vehicles will behave according to the ethics programmed into their software.

The phenomenon of self-learning software leads to the next waste aspect of the new media: "garbage in, garbage out!" In other words, the quality of the input determines the quality of the output. For example, in spring 2016, Microsoft's AI chatbot Tay attempted to learn from people on Twitter. After just a few hours of interaction, @TayandYou was sending racist and sexist tweets and had to be removed from the web. Bad company is a bad influence on artificial intelligence as well. But what happens if you change the bots' nursery? What if you teach them political correctness and social empathy before letting them loose among strangers? Then could they be our friends?

An example of this would be the personal assistant Google Now, which (almost simultaneously with the misconduct of Microsoft's chatbot) expressed its condolences to a user about the death of his father six years before in Nizza when said user wanted to look at his images from Nizza that he had saved in Google Photos. Google Now knows things like this from Gmail, and it reacts in this way because this is how it was programmed.[3] Thrilling philosophical implications can be extrapolated from this anecdote: what happens when artificial intelligence (in the form of a chatbot such as Tay, Google Now, Siri, Jibo, or the algorithm in your car), under the moral control of its programmers, is the source of high-quality contributions to social communication? Instead of being a bad influence on people, can artificial intelligence also improve us?

There are more reasons to begin a primer on new media with the word "waste." One of them leads directly to what in the late 1990s was called "digital literature," and more generally "net culture." *Waste for All: Novel of a Year* (*Abfall für alle: Roman eines Jahres*) was the title of a 1999 book by Rainald Goetz, who would later win the prestigious Büchner Prize. The title was a coy commentary on what a diary is, at least when it's written by someone like Goetz: a textual by-product of everyday experiences, feelings, and thoughts. The literary appeal of this waste product lies in the fact that it wasn't edited retrospectively, as is usually the case with diaries published during the author's lifetime. Goetz's text was published first on the Internet, on the very day it described.

Waste for All was one of the literary Internet projects that was initiated at the close of the twentieth century in order to explore writing under the conditions of the new media, "a pioneering text without avant-garde barriers to understanding," as the cover copy suggested. And in fact, it was simply text, without hyperlinks or multimedia additions. The only change that the new medium of the Internet brought to the old genre of the diary was the shortening of the path to publication, with the promise of greater authenticity. That's no small change, especially for this genre. Since the text went online right away, it was no longer possible to smooth out the entry long after midnight when you came home from a party drunk and irritated, sitting at the computer with one last beer. And since every change to the text can be tracked, the diary also couldn't escape the Internet as a printed book.

Goetz's real-time diary was the innocuous kick-off of live diaries in German, which spoke of everything imaginable, but especially of death. Weblogs were begun with an author's cancer diagnosis or that of their partner, and ended with their death, which was sometimes announced as a suicide. Attempts to give the suffering a face. Attempts to feel a final form of sovereignty in writing, where others feel like "waste" because life has cast them aside. Online encounters with strangers, and with others who are affected by the same problem, or simply moved. An expansion of the space of communication, which such blows of fate had drastically reduced until then. These are the *other* social networks that the Internet makes possible, beyond self-marketing and mutual "likes," beyond the shamelessly happy selfies and the unbearably banal small talk: a place that will catch you when you fall.

All of this doesn't remotely exhaust the framework of meaning associated with waste in the context of the new media. In August 2000, nearly simultaneously with Goetz's diary, a Dutch man, Alex van Es, began to list all of his garbage on his website icepick.com, running everything that he threw away across a barcode scanner. This informational garbage can is the forerunner of the intelligent garbage can that researchers at the University of Newcastle are building. It reports its contents to the garbage collection service, who can then better coordinate their efforts.[4] No one will be surprised to learn that the city government is interested in such data, so that they can better teach their residents how to correctly sort their garbage and recycling. What began as a nerd idea—which included other monitoring systems, such as reporting how often the toilet was flushed and other details of van Es's daily life—became a surveillance technology fifteen years later, which will perhaps become obligatory in another ten years.

This transformation is a shift from an avant-gard-esque project of unreserved self-representation (another example is the American Jennifer Ringley, a nineteen-year-old student who began to post nonstop uncensored images of herself from all of the rooms of her apartment in 1996 at jennicam.com) to one of a global culture of self-marketing on commercial platforms like Facebook, which has caused many pioneers and advocates to lose their former faith in Internet culture. After the "critical turn" in new media studies in the early twenty-first century, the slogan was no longer "information wants to be free" but "information needs protection." The initial praise of the Internet's (individual) freedoms and (democratic) possibilities has given way to critique of its negative aspects: surveillance, narcissism, collective loneliness, self-tracking, the filter bubble, algorithmic regulation—to say nothing of dangerous side effects such as hyper attention, power browsing, addiction to instant gratification, and "fear of missing out" (FOMO). The fact that this original utopia went to waste is the most painful sense in which to read the title of this book.

Just as a by-product is separated from its source and eventually takes on a life of its own, another form of splitting is pertinent to this book in a very particular, methodical, and linguistic way: the break with a style of scholarship, one that may have validity in many senses, but which will not be used here.

Concepts are considered a product of reason, if not its triumph, and they are. But that does not imply the inverse, that reason only exists where people have succeeded or at least tried to precisely describe reality, life, or being—whatever you want to call totality.

Hans Blumenberg's *Theorie der Unbegrifflichkeit* (*Theory of Nonconceptuality*) begins with these words, which contrast the focus of contemporary thought on truth and reasoning with a defense of the incomprehensible, the metaphorical, and the narrative.[5] Blumenberg has not written a condemnation of rationality, but rather has provided a correction to it. Because even if reason's intention has something to do with the potency of concepts, "there is no identity between reason and concept." In other words, to prevent the concept from hindering reason's aspirations, it must possess enough "leeway for everything concrete that is supposed to be subject to its classification."[6]

Blumenberg's plea for the nonconceptual openness of the thinking process has its roots in his previous thought on metaphorology, which viewed metaphor as only "the front line of concept formation, as a makeshift in situations in which technical terminology has not yet been consolidated" but rather as "authentic potency" for registering connections.[7] In both texts quoted above—and with the narrative style of his entire body of work—Blumenberg positions himself as a representative of a lifeworld hermeneutics opposed to theoretical schools, which ensnare the process of theoretical curiosity in methodical and terminological constraints, and which themselves often wither in the process. The "courage of [the mind's] conjectures," which the mind demonstrates by means of metaphors, and the call for openness of thought through a corresponding nonconceptuality both have their roots in the practices of Siegfried Kracauer and Walter Benjamin, who also attempted to capture the cultural upheavals of their era vividly and with bold thinking in their "miniatures"—as Andreas Huyssen terms their style.[8]

Theodor Adorno provides a theoretical validation of such a process. Despite his occasional critique of vague metaphors and analogies, he rejects the "pre-critical job of definition" as a demand "to eliminate the irritating and dangerous elements" "through fixating manipulations of the meanings of concepts."[9] The consciousness of non-identity, which Adorno seeks to heighten in his *Negative Dialectic*, corresponds to the form of the essay—"radically un-radical in refraining from any reduction to a principle"—which "freely associates what can be found associated in the freely chosen object."[10] In the essay, the thinker becomes "an arena of intellectual experience, without simplifying it"; the essay proceeds "methodically unmethodically"; it is not "a down-payment on future syntheses"; on the contrary, it "swallows up the theories that are close by"; it doesn't want to get to the point, and certainly not from a firm perspective, but rather tends "toward the liquidation of opinion, even that from which it takes its own impulse."[11]

Adorno was aware that, particularly in Germany, such an essay "provokes resistance because it is reminiscent of the intellectual freedom" that was not subordinated to the authorities of "sealed and flawlessly organized science"— what Foucault would later refer to as the discourse police.[12] "The essay is the form of the critical category of our mind," says Adorno quoting Max Bense, because to be critical means to make things visible anew and in a different way.[13]

Blumenberg, Adorno, and Bense are proof that the focus of German intellectual culture on conceptual clarity and theoretical stringency wasn't simply relativized by French and American authors, but at times questioned itself from within its own ranks. The opening of thought that these three German philosophers and philosophers of science (further examples being Walter Benjamin and Paul Feyerabend) pursued forty or fifty years ago contended *avant la lettre* for the theoretical legacy of the postmodern, for which conceptual narrowness and theoretical monocultures posed not just an epistemological but a moral problem, and for which the lived variety of perspectives was the practice that accompanied theory. This book is indebted to this legacy— and this dissent from the usual is perhaps the most important interpretation of its title.

A primer is aimed at beginners to impart the ability to read. Correspondingly, a primer for media imparts the ability to read media, that is, media literacy or media education. The typical intended audience of a primer necessarily determines its methodological procedure of representing complex issues in as simple a way as possible. In his 2007 *Das*

ABC der Medien, Norbert Bolz commits himself to this approach, systematically avoiding academic jargon and discreetly placing academic accessories at the end of the book. Both decisions were taken up in the primer you see before you.

Matters are otherwise regarding Bolz's promise to simplify complicated issues. Unlike Bolz's *ABC*, this book is dedicated to the complexity of seemingly simple issues. It aims to listen in on the paradoxical logic of the more or less established phenomena of our digital lifeworld, and to expose their secret connections and concealed consequences. The texts gathered in this book resist the "spell of beginnings"[14] by turning their object over again and again, walking around it as if it were a sculpture, observing it from various angles, and, as if it were a witticism, establishing unexpected connections. They are headlights that illuminate things for a moment. They take hold even of things that can hardly be grasped.

The result is essays that go beyond the obvious and, in foolhardy or reckless fashion, attempt to fathom the wealth of associations in the topics they address. Essays that aim to foster the legibility of the digital revolution that is underway—and which abide by Bense's statement transmitted by Adorno: "He writes essayistically who writes while experimenting, who turns his object this way and that, who questions it, feels it, tests it, thoroughly reflects on it, attacks it from different angles, and in his mind's eye collects what he sees, and puts into words what the object allows to be seen under the conditions established in the course of writing."[15]

WASTE

1 THE QUESTION OF GUILT: TRUMP AND ZUCKERBERG

Did Facebook really make Trump possible? Who belongs to his secret "Facebook army"? How much of the guilt falls on Zuckerberg? And what about Twitter? The media fell all over themselves to point the finger, turning every scrap into a story. They accused Facebook of spreading lies in Trump's favor, providing a gathering place for his supporters, and making it possible for him to reach them. They feverishly tried to hold social media responsible for Trump's victory, after having unscrupulously fawned over the forty-fifth president themselves, back when he was merely one ridiculed but scandalous (and therefore ratings-boosting) candidate among many.

Then everyone was talking about the filter bubble, which cocoons Facebook users in a like-minded circle. This bubble ultimately produced so many hateful comments and violent threats that the Office of the Munich Public Prosecutor opened preliminary investigation proceedings against Zuckerberg for allegedly aiding and abetting hate speech. In doing so, they assumed that Facebook holds a certain influence over society, which it definitely does, but they accused the right people of the wrong thing.

You can hardly reproach Zuckerberg for fake news or bringing together those in the wrong. All the rash accusations, which extend to Trump publicity posted by

Macedonian youths, nearly make a person want to come to Zuckerberg's defense. And yet, the suspicion remains that Facebook paves the way for demagogues like Trump, simply by virtue of the fact that it is what it is. If public discourse were to open an investigation into Zuckerberg—and it absolutely should, at least as a thought experiment to better understand our media society—its charge against him would have to be inciting the people to stupidity rather than inciting them to hate speech. The prosecution's chief witness would still be the filter bubble, but for different reasons than you might think.[1]

FACEBOOK AS FILTER BUBBLE

Facebook didn't invent the filter bubble, of course. The human desire for cognitive consistency has been among the basic insights of psychology since the 1950s. Long before Facebook, we already knew that the control the Internet gives people over their communication processes doesn't really do them any good. Facebook's much-derided algorithms basically just improve on human impulse by means of technology—at least if you reduce the filter bubble to its content.[2]

The problem of the filter bubble is bigger than generally accepted because the bubble is bigger than you think. It contains all the little bubbles the media were so eager to talk about: right-wing and left-wing bubbles, Brexit and anarchist bubbles, bubbles for neoliberals and Marxists, Slavoj Žižekists, and probably even one for postmodernists. The filter bubble is as big as Facebook itself because it doesn't exist *on* but rather *as* Facebook; Facebook is the bubble. In other words, the bubble is a framework of technical and social conditions that largely determine the communication that occurs in its area of influence. Quantity, dualism, and speed are the pillars of this framework.

QUANTITY

Quantity is the currency of the popular, which rules Facebook. We judge the value of the people and posts we see there based on their number of friends, shares, and likes. The question isn't which friends, or what the likes were for, but rather how many. The opportunity for written comments doesn't help much, since (1) they usually only amount to a few words; (2) their number pales in comparison to single-click assessments; and (3) anyone who has ever posted a nuanced text on Facebook knows that they get very few likes. Numerical appraisal is the standard on Facebook, with dubious consequences for politics.

Reduced complexity and automatic judgment can only be avoided with language, because only those who express their own opinions in language ask themselves which words are best suited for the task. It's no guarantee—comments generally devolve into absurdity and insult—but it is the precondition for forming a critical opinion beyond knee-jerk partisanship. "When they go low, we go high," said Michelle Obama during the election campaign in reference to Trump. A powerful statement that nonetheless promises to rise above the level of slogans. A hopeless prospect, if quality is determined in numbers instead of words. When the highest number is what counts, the "low" always comes out on top.

Numeric populism is related to postfactual emotionalism: unjustified likes are the technical version of the mantra-like repetition of empty assertions. Just as a lie that is told often enough in real life becomes a truth for many, a Facebook post gains credence if it is given credence. People always click on the option with the highest number, reinforcing its top status. The number is an emotional plea, because so many can't be wrong, especially if your best friends are among them.

DUALISM

The basic principle of the filter bubble is antagonistic: someone or something belongs or doesn't belong. The opposition connotes inside/outside or us/them thinking at every possible position on the political spectrum. This antagonism is reminiscent of binary code, which is the basis for the Internet and every computer. But can you blame the interface's back-end 0/1 binary for the polarization trend on its front end? Of course you can, insofar as the computer's operational logic aims to organize information into databases, and reduce opinions to the either-or of a like or dislike button.

The consequences of eliminating complexity are highly political, but it is rehearsed in every interaction, even the most unpolitical, whenever we quickly like or dislike things: books, films, photos, recipes, makeup tips, Tinder dates, and newspaper articles. Whether we express it with a click on a like or dislike button, on a thumbs-up or thumbs-down icon, or by swiping left or right, the attitude is always to pursue one of two possibilities, wordlessly and without justification: yes or no, friend or enemy, true or false, in or out. Gradually, you forget how to count to three.

The theoretical foundation of the thinking machine may be "yes or no," but that doesn't necessarily make it as stupid as many of its users. What the binary model lacks in complexity the computer makes up for in speed, by reducing complicated logical operations to many single steps, each ultimately based on a binary formula. People are slower than computers, and since everything moves so quickly on the Internet, they have less and less time for complicated things. In the end, that keeps them more ensnared in the dualistic mode than binary computers are.

SPEED

The central hallmark of click culture is instantaneousness. Nothing in Facebook's news feed is as old as a post from this morning. Reactions must conform, which is why posts by good friends often receive a like before we've had time to look at them. And since new posts have already accumulated by evening, we hardly have time to process the previous ones. If you know the author, you confirm without scrutiny, developing a culture of partisanship and blind trust that doesn't simply go away when the posts become political.

Speed is also an enemy of depth. When time is short, material that is supposed to garner likes must be short on depth. Since everyone likes to be liked, they filter complexity and seriousness out of their posts. And so the hunger for affirmation Facebook instilled in us produces a glut of intellectual fast food. Dumbing things down out of loneliness is the dialectical flipside of the connectivity Zuckerberg has brought into the world.

THE QUESTION OF GUILT

Zuckerberg defended himself against accusations in the wake of Trump's victory with the claim that Facebook gave umpteen million people the opportunity to form a political opinion in the run-up to the election. This self-congratulation demonstrates how little the accused was troubled by a sense of guilt. In acting this way, he can appeal to those who still cling to the founding myth of the Internet as a tool for emancipation and democracy, and who associate Facebook with the Arab Spring, new communication opportunities for minorities, and various forms of activism-via-click.[3]

It's true that Facebook offers a new gathering space where people can communicate uncensored by the "discourse police." It's also true that Facebook gives all people a voice, not just the "big guys," as Zuckerberg likes to emphasize. But a closer look reveals that this doesn't so much solve the problem as exacerbate it. The means to form and express their opinions that Facebook gives its users dismantle the psychological foundations on which the serious formation of opinion is based.

It isn't just alternative political perspectives that fall by the wayside in Facebook's communication bubble, but also the effort required for something as complicated as politics can be. Complex arguments are jettisoned in favor of simple slogans, text in favor of images, laborious explorations at understanding the world and the self in favor of amusing banalities, deep engagement in favor of the click. Facebook's crime doesn't consist in tolerating fake news and hate speech, but rather in creating conditions for communication that make people susceptible to such posts.

Zuckerberg likes to emphasize that Facebook is not a media company but a tech company, allotting it just as little responsibility for the content shared as Apple has if a murder is planned via iPhone. Critics are right to retort that Facebook has become the only newspaper that many people read, which demands a corresponding level of responsibility for the content presented there. This responsibility entails not treating information impartially as a technology company would, but rather separating news of parliament from that of our best friends, and prioritizing the former over the latter. But the critique has to go further than that and assess more deeply. Facebook isn't just an information provider; it is an institution for socialization that handles information in such a way that actually makes it easier for demagogues like Trump to win—as well as those who will imitate him.

The investigation into Zuckerberg would have to summon more witnesses against Facebook than the filter bubble, and it would have to accuse it of more than quantity, dualism, and speed. Disinformation begins with the range of information in the Facebook bubble, which replaces the political with the private, and replaces intelligence and education with banality and spectacle. Zuckerberg does all he can to expedite this process when he deprives traditional media of subscribers and advertising clients, backing them into a corner economically. He has pushed them so far by now that they grit their teeth and seek refuge on Facebook, courting an audience with "instant articles" like a voice in the wilderness.

But that isn't all. He can be charged with more counts of inciting the people to stupidity. Day after day, click after click, Facebook squanders the mental resources of an educated public: patience, skepticism, concentration, interest, a certain respect for experts, and the willingness to work hard enough to understand them. All of this will be discussed below.

The question of liability must be resolved in the first place, because it is doubtful that *one* man and *one* company have the power to change the world's cultures. The defense will argue, in Zuckerberg's own words, that Facebook is just picking up on trends. The prosecution will be correct to retort that Facebook reinforces or initiates these trends for base motives, sacrificing deep reading for copious clicks simply owing to its business model. The defense will counter the accusation of personal gain by pointing to the Chan Zuckerberg Initiative, which the prosecution ... and so on.

MEDIA EDUCATION

It all blew over in a few weeks. Not fear of Trump, but the allegations against Zuckerberg. The topic was exhausted, according to the press, while media scholars hoped it would finally be explored in depth. Other questions were now causing a stir: Trump's victory as a resounding defeat for political consultants and polling agencies, the significant number of Latinos who voted for Trump, Trump's transition team, his son-in-law. Facebook only made it past the media's news-value filter again when massive ads by Russian agents were detected.

Nevertheless, the anxious probing of Facebook's societal influence, and the clueless superficiality of the criticism made apparent the need for discussion. Now everything depended on keeping the question alive beyond the daily business of the old scandal-oriented media, and to bring it to all corners of society. The criticism must go deeper and gain a broader foothold. It must be developed at universities, it must reach politicians, it must go into the schools, it must lead to media literacy that doesn't just ask how we can effectively use media, but also how new media change the conditions of our existence. What social, cultural, and political consequences does it have? Is that what we want? Can we stop it?

In his first statement on the election results, Zuckerberg explained (under the notable headline "Feeling Hopeful") that his project was larger than any presidency and that progress doesn't occur along a straight line. His mission is to bring people closer together, as he often points out. Facebook isn't supposed to reconcile only Americans; it should unite the world. However, the considerations presented above suggest that the conditions for communication on

Facebook tear the world apart because people are not prepared to handle opposing political views in a constructive way, or to view their own skeptically. Why is Zuckerberg so hopeful? What does he have in mind? Could it be that we've completely misunderstood him up to now? Don't we have to think of the filter bubble in much bigger terms than those used here? Does Zuckerberg want to solve the problem of political aggression by driving the political out of communication? Does he want Facebook to be the enormous party of banalities, free of all explosive political material? To save the world through a culture of the banal—stupidity as remedy? It's an absurd thought, which we'll save for the end of the book.[4]

What thrilling times those were, when Faust made his pact with the devil in order to change the world. Yes, it was also about women. But anyone who has made it past Part I of Goethe's *Faust* knows that the Gretchen story was only the prelude (a delay, certainly, but also an inner preparation) to Faust's real role as a ceaseless, ruthless world-changer. This ambition is already evident in Faust's pact with the devil, which he formulates as a wager: "If ever I plead with the passing moment: / Linger awhile, oh how lovely you are! / Then shut me up in close confinement, / and I'll gladly go to my destruction."[1] Faust is required to give his soul to the devil, in exchange for the latter's services, only if he halts the forward movement of internal and external time—but not so long as he continues to strive, try to understand the secret of what keeps the world going, and attempt to change it.

Does Faust still live? Did the devil come for him in the end? Today, we are probably most likely to find Faust in Silicon Valley, where all kinds of technologies are developed that, as we are constantly reminded, will make the world a better place. In the information age, this generally means improving the flow of information, the form of communication, and the degree of interconnectedness. The Gretchen question of the present is therefore: And how do you feel about Facebook? Which naturally includes the question: How do you feel about the passing moment?

If we turn the question back on ourselves, it looks, at first, as if we were all hopeless losers of Faust's wager. Who still wants to change the world? Who still believes, like Faust (or Adorno), that the history of humankind hasn't even really begun yet? Who among us doesn't constantly hold onto the moment as if it were essential to never let it go? Our devices and Facebook pages are full of photographic witness to beautiful moments, which in the Chinese equivalent WeChat are in fact called "Moments." But: more is less! Along with the number of moments that we hold onto, the suspicion is also growing that something is wrong.

THE BURDENS AND PLEASURES OF THE MOMENT

At least since the proclamation of the "experience society" and "experiential industry" in the 1980s, the postmodern subject has been in hot pursuit of experiences, rather than working toward a goal. Liberated from old structures, traditional role models, and categorically imposed life plans, the subject develops an identity that does not let itself be determined by the past or obligated to the future. It is free to do whatever it wants, without having to want anything and also without knowing what it should want. Thus it lives on, in the delirium of an endless present, ceaselessly underway from moment to moment.

That this radical present-relatedness also creates pressure and anxiety is already announced in the titles of some diagnoses of the contemporary era, for example *Tyranny of* the Moment (2001) or *Present Shock* (2014).[2] But what else should we expect, after the end of history? What role remains for the present, if we no longer believe that it owes the past a better future? No longer part of any historical-philosophical current of history, it floats on air until it is only bearable if we are in motion: from event to event. Without a deeper link to the rest of time, though, every event is always simultaneously not enough and much too much.

The problem is not that in the twenty-first century the moment in time, unlike those experienced by Faust or the Romantics, is no longer an intense experience of the self. The problem is that it no longer even allows the self a moment of intense enjoyment. Life experiences entail an obligation to actually experience them. They demand of us a presence that Faust possessed during every moment that he did not ask to linger. We, on the other hand, think we have done our part if we bring home a souvenir from the museum shop and a video from the rock concert. This has become so bad that meanwhile musicians publicly complain to their fanatically videoing fans: "Could you stop filming me? Because I'm really here in real life, you can enjoy it in real life rather than through your camera."[3]

We are at some particular place only because we don't happen to be someplace else, and we often ask ourselves whether we shouldn't be moving on. We are no longer *Faust II*, but neither are we *Faust I*—that was the wild 1960s, when the thing to do was break the fetters of bourgeois existence and we still assumed we owed this to the world. Generation X already feels relieved of this mandate. As the character

Troy Dyer puts it in the 1994 cult film *Reality Bites*: "I am not under any orders to make the world a better place." Since then we rush breathlessly from one urgency to the next and never actually feel good anywhere. We know this as soon as the world around us accidentally falls silent, for a change. The salvation that now no longer releases us lies in new media and social networks.

NETWORK SMOKE

The smartphone, as they say, is the cigarette of the twenty-first century. This comparison is even more apt if the cigarette is considered not as a luxury item, but as a stopgap—a refuge and means of self-protection whenever we are confronted with an uncomfortable, pressing present. The decisive difference is not so much the dissimilar nature of the object, or its different consequences for our health, as the different social aspect of the flight. While smoking out of embarrassment isolates a person in the here and now, communication with the social network, in the there and now, leads to a kind of group cuddling of sharing and liking. People don't retreat helplessly into their own cloud of smoke; they feel that they are active members of a community to which they can delegate the moment they just experienced the same way others delegate their moments. Through the act of communicating, each person helps the next one disguise her momentary fear as the power to do something.

There is a twofold avoidance of perceiving the moment in time: we flee it as we take it in, and we usually never return to it. Photographic busyness is not a betrayal of the present in the interest of the future, as it was in the past. There are no more slide shows in a circle of relatives, no more solitary, late-night recollections over a glass of wine and a table littered with photographs. Who has time to have a second look at all the photos it once seemed so important to create? Subsequent viewing has ceded its rights to sharing-in-place. The social network is always looking on; it sees for us, while we, for our part, are rifling through the sharings of others, waiting for the first likes.

What to many people looks like a narcissistic need for communication is basically a cry for help to our network friends, who should liberate us from the present moment that, to judge by the photos, is making us so happy. Are the many snapshots on our social networks proof that we are winning the wager after all? Neither Mephistopheles nor the Lord above would support this view.

PARALLEL WORLD

Faust cannot linger because he has so much he wants to do. He must still invent money at the kings' court, spirit Helen away from antiquity, invent artificial man, and win land from the sea. Faust is the "egomaniacal, experience-devouring imperial self." He leaves the moment permanently behind him, because he is moving with the wave of the future. We, on the other hand, are the "narcissistic, infantile, empty self." We are not being driven forward, nor inward, but only somewhere else. The "psychological man" that superseded the "imperial self" in the 1970s has been replaced by the *phatic* one with the same objective: "mental health."[4]

What we are doing, when we hold fast to every moment and simultaneously betray it, is leaping out of time into the communication network of cyberspace. In this way, we who live without past and future also transcend the present. Wherever we may happen to be, in the social space of the digital media we feel safe and secure. There, every app is familiar, every contact a favorite, every threat can potentially be clicked away.

The smartphone is more than a cigarette. It is a protective shield against the rest of the world. Whenever we are fleeing from a moment in time, we flee there. For virtual space is lovely enough to linger in—even more lovely than the moment to which Faust swore he would never yield. The wager, some people say, has long since been lost. We have long since been put in chains, and have long since lost our souls. For digital media, the same people claim, are not the services Mephistopheles provides before we win or lose the wager; they are already his realm.

3 LOSS OF PRIVACY

It's possible that future accounts of history will tell of a dispute that took place in 2023. Back then, they'll say, the German Ministry of the Internet (founded just a few years after the 2013 NSA surveillance scandal) sought an injunction against the Association of Data Privacy Activists. Their so-called white block had long urged people to create pockets of noncommunication, by deactivating the GPS on their smartphones, for example. By 2023, deactivation was no longer possible, but owning a smartphone was not yet required by law. Now the Ministry of the Internet wanted to change that.

The Ministry of Transportation proposed establishing presence technology (which displays the position of your vehicle with an accuracy of five centimeters) in traffic law. That was important, it was said, because cars were now silent. All kinds of collisions could be avoided without seeing or hearing a thing, simply through automatic warning signals and application of the brakes if the distance separating the position coordinates of two objects equipped with such sensors fell below the minimum limit. The data privacy activists had no arguments against this procedure, which seemed safe, but they demanded anonymization, since preventing a collision between a car and a bike doesn't require the operators to be identified.

The Ministry of the Internet did not agree with this perspective, because cutting-edge data mining could calculate the likelihood of a collision based on insights into the operators' physical and mental states, their daily routines, the vehicle models, and other available data, and trigger effective preventative measures accordingly. Since traffic safety is not a personal matter, citizens couldn't refuse to be identified. The appeal to create holes in cybernetic communication was deemed a danger to transportation, even labeled a terrorist act by some, and ultimately prohibited by the judiciary.

SNOWDEN'S DISRUPTION

Science fiction? What part of it? Presence technology and smart things are now just as much a topic in the newspapers as the use of GPS is a widespread reality. Algorithms have long been poring over big data for hidden connections, more and more self-trackers willingly contribute to the data pool with observations about their own daily behavior, and rationalizations were a tool of modern state governance long before the digitization of society. Is it science fiction that people will soon tell their wearables to find information about the people sitting at the next table over?

When Google Glass was about to be introduced to the market, a blog comment prophesied that the wearers of such surveillance devices would have higher insurance premiums because of all of the injuries and broken noses they could expect from their surroundings. *That* is a fiction. On the contrary, Google Glass—or whatever the marketable equivalent will be called—will be as successful as the iPad, and its users will receive all sorts of discounts if they let the insurance companies look through their lenses.

The NSA scandal turned data privacy into a news topic during the 2013 summer slump, and Orwell's *1984* into vacation reading. Cries to save basic civil rights and the Internet as it once was (a place for free expression of opinion, without surveillance or commerce) put many people in a fighting mood. Few comments emphasized that loss of data privacy was only in part a product of the secret services; ignorance, avarice, and convenience are stronger factors.

COLLABORATIONS

It is ignorant to say, "But I don't have anything to hide." Who knows what patterns the algorithms will find in your behavior, and the degree to which these might be a disadvantage? How can you exercise your basic right to informational self-determination if modern analysts don't even tell you what they've discovered, nor ask you if they can make public use of it?

Such a statement also lacks solidarity, which is made clear by a report about the first marriage between two men in a Protestant church in Germany in August 2013, right at the peak of the privacy debate that followed Snowden's revelation. What was forbidden or taboo twenty years ago is now recognized by society and blessed by the church, so that many who yesterday had something to hide are now considered to have been good people all along. Anyone who sings the hymn of transparency turns a cold shoulder to the troubles of minorities, and they are politically naive because, on the one hand, they assume that their society's current laws and moral attitudes are up to date, and on the other hand, that they are sacrosanct. Jews also once thought that they had now arrived in mainstream German society, and after Trump's victory, many US citizens fear that they will be driven back out of their society's mainstream again. As long as history cannot protect progress against setbacks, it must be the duty of all citizens to protect the right to hide things by practicing it themselves.

It also demonstrates a lack of solidarity when you hand over your personal data for financial gain. It starts when you divulge individual consumer habits in exchange for discounts, or allow Google's complimentary email service to read your correspondence. Anyone who pockets insurance rebates because they allow their driving style or body movements to be monitored ultimately see to it that those who exceed the calculated average (or don't want to provide proof of their averageness) must pay more. Personal permissiveness with data has consequences for others.

But the most powerful engine for loss of data privacy is convenience, the delegation of as many tasks as possible to software-equipped everyday objects that communicate with one another: the swimming pool that heats itself when a barbecue is on the calendar, the refrigerator that places orders when the beer is gone or the milk is expired, the car that checks traffic updates and construction schedules to automatically adjust the route. The media scholar Marshall

McLuhan termed the media an "extension of man." There are extensions for the arms (hammers, pistols), the legs (bicycles, cars), the eye (telescopes, microscopes), the memory (writing, photography). The Internet of things allows computers not just to compute for us, but also to observe and evaluate our environment, that is, to think. It is unsurprising that for McLuhan, the shadow of the extension of man is amputation; we know that driving cars doesn't make our legs any stronger. The Internet of things doubles these shadows. It doesn't make our thinking any more resilient, and it functions all the better the more it knows about us.

THE POWERLESSNESS OF SUCCESS

The communication of things, history "books" of the future will tell us, was a triumph of artificial intelligence and human convenience over the remaining efforts at data privacy in the early twenty-first century. It made human life easier, and also easier to control because it subjects nearly every action to data analysis. A paradise for doctors, city planners, and traffic controllers. The resulting big data pool is not a symptom of a zealous secret service, but rather the legacy of the Enlightenment, which viewed every unmeasured hill as an insult to reason. Society's digitization is the extension of this yardstick into the social.

Loss of data privacy is thus the product of a cultural and technological disposition, which in McLuhan's perspective is identified as second-order technical determinism: "We shape our tools, and thereafter our tools shape us." It's an old story: machines take command, like the supercomputer HAL in Stanley Kubrick's *2001: A Space Odyssey.* A sort of "Sorcerer's Apprentice 2.0," except that unlike in Goethe's ballad, the master also doesn't know how to get rid of the spirits he's summoned.

In his 1979 book, *The Imperative of Responsibility: In Search of an Ethics for the Technological Age*, the philosopher of technology Hans Jonas described the problem as powerlessness in the face of success: the catastrophe for humanity is the triumph of *homo faber*, the maker, who ultimately becomes "the compulsive executor of his capacity." In summer 2013, "YES WE SCAN" was written on a poster protesting the NSA's surveillance practices, which, together with the famous phrase that accompanied President Obama into office, characterizes the fatal relationship of modernity to technology: yes we can analyze big data better and better, and we do.

RAISON D'ÉTAT

Have we already been defeated by these technical capacities—"programming" or "analyzing" in current terms—or can we still escape the power that we have over algorithms before they force their postulates on us? The answer also depends on the consciousness of the problem that the weakening of data protection leaves behind, and where people suspect the enemy might lie: in the secret service and the state, in the Internet giants and programmers, or in ourselves, since (for example) accident prevention through algorithms is such a relief to us that we don't just accept the necessary exposure, but also force it on the remaining "enemies of progress."

Government ministries also recognized long ago that collecting data makes their work much easier. Though the 2016 "Law on Digitizing the Energy Transition" (*Gesetz zur Digitalisierung der Energiewende*) enacted by the German Bundestag doesn't compel identification via presence technology, it does promote the installation of smart electricity meters. This will generate energy savings, so the justification goes, of at least 1.5 percent. Who would want to bring up data privacy—as the Green Party and Left Party did when they voted against the law—in opposition to ecological successes, or mention pedantic security risks because, as an interface to the "smart home," smart meters could allow unwarranted access to it?

As one politician from the center-left Social Democratic Party put it, the old "uncommunicative" technology of electromechanical meters must finally be replaced with digital technology. A politician from the center-right Christian Democratic Union affirmed this longing for technological progress: "We can't always keep holding ourselves back with data privacy."[1] Occurrences like these make it clear that loss of data privacy is neither science fiction nor something that democratically elected parliaments would rather leave to dictatorial systems.

4 THE FATEFUL YEAR 1984

Some years, long before the dawn of the actual New Year, carry a burden whose weight increases steadily between January and December. The first millennium was a case in point, as a thousand years after the birth of Christ humanity succumbed to an end-time mood. The relief over the fact that the Antichrist and the Last Judgment failed to appear can still be seen today in the many churches that were constructed during the endless year 1000. The year 1984 is another example of the symbolic power of some years' dates, and this one was especially foreboding.

The all-clear came on a TV show from WNET, recorded on New Year's Day in New York and Centre Pompidou in Paris, which was also broadcast in Germany and South Korea, reaching ten million people worldwide. The show was created by Nam June Paik—the father of media art, originally from Seoul—and was fearlessly titled *Good Morning, Mr. Orwell*.[1] "What you are about to see," the cheerful moderator George Plimpton greeted the audience, "are positive and interactive uses of electronic media, which Mr. Orwell, the first media prophet, never predicted. This is a New Year's celebration which could only happen with television."

The carefree tone persisted throughout the program, which featured heroes of the avant-garde such as Laurie

Anderson, Peter Gabriel, John Cage, Allen Ginsberg, Merce Cunningham, and Joseph Beuys, along with the New Wave band Oingo Boingo performing their song "Wake Up (It's 1984)," with lines like:

> Big brother's watching, we watch him back
> We see right through his disguise
> He tries to scare us, with angry words
> But we all know that they're lies.

There was only one moment during the show when the tone shifted, when the French performer Sapho sang "Big Brother is not watching you / But TV is eating up your brains." A different fear emerged, which had hardly been noted up to that point; a shift that seemed inevitable, at least in Germany, in which January 1, 1984, also marked the beginning of commercial television stations with no educational mandate. From this perspective, there was no reason to give the all-clear, either on January 1 or on December 31, 1984.

BIG BROTHERS

"On January 24, Apple Computer will introduce Macintosh, and you'll see why 1984 won't be like *1984*." This was the announcement that was made in the famous advertisement Apple produced for the Super Bowl on January 22, 1984. The text appeared following a race between a group of armed men and a woman carrying a sledgehammer. As the sledgehammer demolishes a screen from which a man is haranguing a crowd of faceless figures, a murmur of wonder runs through the crowd and light floods the scene. The book *1984* was George Orwell's novel about a totalitarian state. Referring to it seemed natural in 1983, even if just then, at the dawn of neoliberalism, there were absolutely no signs that the feared event might take place. The only Big Brother who existed in 1983, for the countries of Eastern Europe, was the Soviet Union, which was about to announce Glasnost and Perestroika.

For Apple, however, the face of the enemy was not a dictator at all. It was an economic competitor: IBM, familiarly known as Big Blue. The advertising clip was using a cannon to shoot at a fly. From a political perspective, even a big corporation like IBM is nothing compared to an authoritarian system—at least until Apple itself became a corporation and created its own "iCulture," with which it essentially set the terms of social communication, from the "lock-in effect" to the censorship it imposed at its app store. But even if, in 1983, there was no Thought Police for Apple to swing a sledgehammer at, the company's liberation rhetoric had a rational core: if computing power is real power, then the affordable personal computer equals the empowerment of the individual. How effective, we ask, three decades after 1984, is the computer in everyone's hand against the things that are symbolized in *1984*?

That something has gone awry is already illustrated by Germany's Big Brother Awards, which Apple has received twice since 1983: in 2011, for "dubious data protection guidelines," and again in 2013, for "comprehensive video surveillance of employees at Apple stores in Germany."[2] Okay, unwanted awards like these can happen to anyone.

Even the art fair Ars Electronica received the Austrian Big Brother Award in 2001, for "belittling biometrics." And the files on the other Internet giants have grown just as fat. Google, for example, received the Austrian Big Brother Award in 2012, and the German one in 2013, for "global data hunger."

More exciting than attacks by antitechnology groups is when the major corporations accuse each other of Big Brotherhood. This occurred implicitly on February 6, 2011, in another Super Bowl ad, in which Motorola compared its Android XOOM tablet to Apple's iPad. The promise was huge this time, too: "The tablet to create a better world."[3] The tagline follows a short film, which once again shows a big crowd of people with expressionless faces marching in formation, this time dressed not in gray but in shining white, and each plugged into an iPod. Only one figure, reading *1984* on his tablet, is wearing dark clothes and later, at the office, produces an animated bouquet of flowers for one of the white-robed figures, whose wonder-filled gaze at the new device recalls an earlier ad for the Macintosh.

This short film functions only if it is read ironically and the reader is familiar with the backstory, for the promise of creating a better world with this tablet can only be understood in reference to Apple's promise that it could prevent *1984* with the Macintosh. Why a "better" world, and why power to the people (the title of the film is "Empower the People")? That there can be no answer to this—nothing but a sentimental love story between a figure in dark clothing and a figure in white—is the actual point. Motorola unmasks the pathos, which in the Apple ad was still serious, by exaggerating it and exercising self-criticism, basically saying: "Apple once claimed it wanted to save the world, but it only wants to sell its products; we don't want anything else either, but at least we admit it."

What Motorola attempted without much success in 2011, when it challenged Apple's monopoly of the tablet market, Google tried to do for its Android system in the smartphone market. When this set it on a collision course with Apple, Google explained the offensive at its Developers' Conference in 2010 by citing the need to avoid a draconian future in which the only choice would be "one man, one company, one device, one carrier"—and showed an image in which the date 1984 appeared under the tag line "Not the Future we Want."[4] The rhetoric was a subtle jibe at Apple's video, where Big Brother had shouted from the screen: "We are one people. With one will. One resolve. One cause." Naturally, Google's open source operating system is the better alternative over Apple's closed system. But Google is no less intent than Apple on achieving the monopolist's "lock-in effect"—ideologically it too is a Big Brother, whose last words in the video are "We shall prevail!"

When it comes to surveillance, moreover, there are not many good things to be said about a business that boasts that nothing on the Internet can be hidden from it. A promise of this type is, of course, integral to the very nature of the product that made "Google" into a verb. For we expect, of a search engine, that it will find whatever it is asked to find. But somehow it does sound threatening when then CEO Eric Schmidt proudly announces, in 2010: "We know where you are. We know where you've been. We can more or less know what you're thinking about."[5] It sounds threatening for another reason, too, because in effect this knowledge is not confined to Googling. Google's email is also read by Google's algorithms, and now there are Google's Cloud Platform, with which data that previously sat on personal computers wanders off to central servers (a super gift for secret services, hackers and any future Big Brother regime). And there is (if it comes to this) Google Glass, which allows even one's own gaze to be observed.

There is another, ancillary irony in the fact that even Paul Buchheit, the Google employee to whom Google owes its unofficial company motto "Don't be evil," himself played quite intensely with the devil, first by inventing Gmail and then, in 2007, by launching his own startup, FriendFeed, a social networking service that made it possible for users to follow the Internet activities of their friends: to see what they post, what music they listen to, and the like. When Facebook bought FriendFeed for $50 million in 2009, the site ended up with the Internet's youngest Big Brother, who makes sure that our entire life, more or less, is exposed to observation.

To round out the story: Facebook received the German Big Brother Award in 2011, for "targeted research of people and their personal relationships," and the Austrian Big Brother Award in both 2014, for "psycho-experiments with its members," and 2015, "for the patent that is intended to enable credit-scoring of the user's friends." Facebook founder Mark Zuckerberg doesn't understand all the fuss over data protection and informational self-determination: after all, if a person has nothing to hide, he also has nothing to fear. For this level of Big Brother logic, at the Austrian Big Brother Awards of 2011 he deservedly received the "Special prize for 'lifelong nuisance.'"

DOUBLE NEGATION

In fact, *1984* did not happen and will never happen, nor will *1985*, at least in the form in which Anthony Burgess described it in his 1978 novel of that name: as a totalitarian regime of labor unions that terrorize the land with strikes and drive strike-breakers to their doom. After the neoliberal turn and the Cold War, we need to go back some years before Orwell to find a model for the future, in Aldous Huxley's novel *Brave New World*. Written in 1932 under the influence of the Roaring Twenties and Pavlovian behavioral conditioning, this was a more refined dystopia: a dystopia without complaining, one that its "victims," in their hedonism, didn't even recognize as such. In 1985, Neil Postman's essay "Amusing Ourselves to Death," inspired by television culture, proclaimed Huxley's vision to be the more likely model for the future.

The "telly" also plays a central role in Burgess's *1985*, in which the half-witted teen-age daughter of the rebellious hero has only three things in her head: eating, watching television, and masturbating. Burgess is still entirely in

Orwell's debt when he portrays ideological indoctrination with a hodgepodge of history and the use of degraded language, now dubbed "Workers' English." Postman's essay, on the other hand, shows why the future will look like neither 1985 nor 1984, but like Huxley's satanic promise of permanent contentment. In Huxley, the drug Soma destroys the need for critical thinking, while in Postman it is television that performs this function. "Public Discourse in the Age of Show Business," as the subtitle of Postman's essay reads, is not manipulated by a "consciousness industry"[6] that implants specific thoughts in the subject, the way Burgess portrayed it in his novel *A Clockwork Orange*, for example. Television is a zero-sum medium that wants nothing more than for people to be amused. The formula is domestication through dumbing down. As Adorno once wrote, "The liberation that amusement promises is freedom from thinking as negation."[7] The objective is to keep viewers continuously occupied so they don't come up with "wrong ideas." This negation of negation becomes radical when it is liberated from the television in the living room. The cornerstone was laid in the year 1984, when Apple's Macintosh and Facebook's Zuckerberg first saw the light of day.

FOMO SOMA

"Never trust a computer you can't lift." This is how Steve Jobs advertised the Macintosh. Since then, the devices have grown ever smaller. Today, we hold them casually in one hand while our thumb roams through all the amusements in the world. The new Soma is FOMO (fear of missing out). It ensures that, amid all the communication we are engaged in, we can hardly find time to think. Television is always with us, thanks, first of all, to the iPhone; and Zuckerberg's Facebook ensures it always has something exciting on offer.

Big Brothers love little devices, especially when they are ubiquitous. When even the dust is full of software and all things communicate with each other, no facet of life will remain that is not turned into data, that is, made analyzable and controllable. The control will present itself as love and support, the same way Microsoft, in the summer of 2015, tried to offer us its new operating system Windows 10, which wants to know every single thing you do on the computer and the Internet—the better, we are told, to protect its users from cybercrime. A bold move, so soon after Snowden, but one that could end up winning, for since 9/11 the business of security in exchange for transparency is doing very well.

This brave new world will not be able to do without surveillance, but the latter will occur in our interest and we ourselves will install it each time. For in fact, as long as we are nicely amusing ourselves with Facebook, WhatsApp, Snapchat, Instagram, or whatever, there is nothing fear. The much-lamented dumbing down through those media is no unwanted side effect. It is also important in Huxley, where oxygen is withheld from the embryos of the "Epsilons" (the caste used for lower-level tasks) in order to keep them intellectually limited. Naturally, in the twenty-first century this does not take such a drastic form. Instead of oxygen denial there is now information surplus, its permanence ensured by the smartphone. The more incisive anti-film to Apple's "1984" would give the men iPhones as weapons, which they would try to force upon the woman they race against. The woman would have the features of Steve Jobs, who, as we know, kept his own children away from iPhones.[8] For the worst are those who publicly preach wine and drink water in private.

5 LIFE AS AN ARCHIVE

Those were the days, when nothing ever got lost. There was no human action that didn't contribute to world history, which in turn, was viewed as nothing but constant improvement. Immanuel Kant based his "Idea for a Universal History with a Cosmopolitan Purpose" on this phenomenon, seeking a historian who would look at the "senseless course of human events" and recognize the deeper "purpose in nature" as the *a priori* of philosophical millenarianism.[1]

Kant's essay was published at the end of 1784 in a monthly Berlin journal. The historian Kant was looking for, his one-time student Johann Gottfried Herder, had already proclaimed ten years earlier in his essay *This Too a Philosophy of History for the Formation of Humanity*: "As now since the creation of our earth no ray of sun is lost on it, so also no fallen leaf of a tree, no flown seed of a plant, no mouldering animal carcass, and even less so does *a single* action by a living being remain without effect."[2]

How different all of that is today! Gone is the conviction that everything that happens has a deeper meaning, faded are the great tales of human history led by reason to a society of free people on free soil. Even individuals now see their lives as a mere sequence of unrelated life situations, in which they're never really at home. Under such conditions, depictions of history and the self flee into the archive.

COMPLETENESS AND ORDER

If there's a gun hanging on the wall, it should go off. Thus, the Russian writer Anton Chekhov illustrated the fundamental law of purpose-oriented narration in 1889. The elements of the narrative fabric must functionally justify their presence, which naturally doesn't mean that a gun that appears again and again but never goes off remains meaningless in a story.

This is true of traditional narration theory, and it isn't any different in the narrative writing of history. In 1776, the Göttingen historian Johann Christoph Gatterer explained in his programmatic text *On the Historical Plan and the Amalgamation of Stories Based upon It:* "Events which do not belong to the system are for the writer of history no events at all, so to speak."[3] When Herder postulated what might be termed his "law of conservation of energy in history," others were soon convinced that what it really meant was: everything is related, but only if it is carefully preselected. Narrative is the enemy of everything that falls outside of it, the complete opposite of an archive.

Unlike the narrating historian, the collecting archivist is an ally of the facts, which they accumulate without regard for perspective. They aren't concerned with the order of the whole, but rather with representative completeness. It is no coincidence that we gained new respect for this posture at the end of the twentieth century, once the grand narratives seemed exhausted. In the same year that Francis Fukuyama declared the end of history, the French historical theorist Pierre Nora identified a "cult of continuity," in which memory's "new vocation is to record; delegating to the archive the responsibility of remembering."[4]

This outsourcing of remembering to the archive means replacing one's personal relationship to what has happened with neutral recording of what has passed. It is neutral because it is without passion and it does justice to detail because it has no narrative plan whatsoever. This is also precisely what is happening today with social media.

FORGETFUL RECORDING

The more life takes place in and by means of digital media, the more it takes place in the archive. Be it emails, WhatsApp messages, status updates, comments, likes, or shares on social networks, the basic approach is always to preserve. Everything that is to be forgotten must also be deleted. At the same time, the archive itself is the medium of forgetting if it preserves events not because they were meaningful to us, but simply because they happened.

Communicating our lives has become episodic and system-less. We produce status updates that hardly relate to one another and can't even be linked to each other within Facebook's interface. We chronicle events whose deeper meaning for us we neither know nor explore, if we're not deeply aware of their meaninglessness beyond that particular moment anyway. Strictly speaking, we don't even chronicle what *has* happened anymore, we just record what *is* happening. A quick photo of an event, shared on the spot. Seconds later, the first feedback arrives. So we fill our personal archive with selfies, food porn, and other snapshots, without ever having to relate the collected incidents to each other.

The highly symbolic device made just for this process is the Narrative Clip, a small camera worn at the collar that automatically takes pictures every thirty seconds, using these photos to condense the day's "narrative." It is a narrative in the spirit of the archive, selective only with regard to the quality of the photos, without any tactical narrative discrimination toward isolated events and without any guilty conscience about guns that haven't gone off.

THE ELIMINATION OF THE ARCHIVE

Of course, the work of remembrance can also happen later. An archive has all the time in the world. It is as patient as it is reliable, saving everything until we want to look back through our streams of data on WhatsApp or query our Facebook timelines about ourselves. But do we really want that? Do we have the time and the courage to engage with our former selves? Nothing prevents us from interacting with a medium in an optimal way—besides media use habits, which are hard to shake.

At the end of history and narratives, isn't the truest and most honest consequence the end of the archive itself? The app that perfects this step is Snapchat. It became popular because it promised to destroy the photos sent via it, and it remained popular even after screenshot software undermined the assurance of destruction. More important than having control over one's own image was that it didn't fill an archive with photos taken and received. Snapchat is *the* technology for the presentism of our time. The lived moment is not preserved, even as it is retained. The point is not to remember this moment later via a photo, but rather to share it with others now. The camera went from a media for overcoming time to one of collapsing space. In a way, it turned into a telescope, with the result that it has shifted radically to become even more of a medium of the banal.

Even the things saved in the "My Story" function on Snapchat disappear after twenty-four hours, very much unlike a diary or the Facebook timeline. Nothing more aptly embodies the episodic, situative identity of the post- or late modern—which sees each day in its uniqueness instead of understanding it as a building block in a life story—than an app that saves nothing, allowing every morning to begin anew. This tenet is also supported by the absence of a "like" function in Snapchat: strategic photography loses meaning if you can't build popularity.

THE TWILIGHT OF MEMORY

The technical configuration of Snapchat isn't without its irony. While the digital archive is a form of forgetting, the archive's self-destruction demands the return of memory. When Snapchatters go through their own or other people's "stories" in the evening, saving the images that are important to them in spite of it all, they are carrying out a selection of the events, musing on their continuing significance, which gets lost during the day's frenzy of sharing.

Of course, there is already an app for that too: 1 Second Everyday lets you create a montage of the best seconds of every day. The images selected form a kind of secondary memory. Although we do not (unconsciously) retain in our memories those experiences that were truly meaningful, we at least (consciously) select the ones that now seem most important to us from the heap of accumulated photos.

Underneath it all, the algorithms are spinning out new stories. Equipped with even the tiniest detail, with even the most isolated event, they canvass the big data pool for hidden correlations, as Kant, Herder, and Gatterer once canvassed history. The grand narrative they are working on is characterized by a completely new philosophy that, in allusion to those texts from long ago, could be termed the ubiquitous story of humanity with a cybernetic purpose.

6 THE DIGITAL MADELEINE

A few years ago, when a friend who has since died gave me a book of "what-if" questions, I immediately put them to good use and asked him: If you could receive a telegram from a person in history, who would it be and what would the telegram say? His response: Rainer Maria Rilke with an invitation to dinner at Duino Castle. Since then, I always think of this friend when I think of Rilke, which happens more frequently than I think of my friend, which naturally also always makes me think of Rilke. What I know about this friend today is the result of an imaginary moment that followed a fantasy question: I see him strolling to the Golfo die Trieste with Rilke, talking about loneliness in life and especially in love relationships; I recognize him by the words that I, in my imagination, put in his and Rilke's mouths.

The answer to my question that day, a long time ago, turned Rilke into the madeleine that reliably reminds me of the friend. I refer here to Marcel Proust's madeleine, which, dunked in tea and ingested, reawakens memories of the childhood of the narrator in Proust's novel *In Search of Lost Time*. This provides an old-fashioned contrast to the ultra-modern memory activators of the social media. While the madeleine, involuntarily, literally provokes the memory in the interior of the subject, in the framework of social media the activators are as external to the person who is remembering as, basically, the memories that are being invoked. They are the counterpart to the automatized world and the narrative of the self on which they draw.

MAKING HISTORY

The Facebook function "On This Day" reminds us of what we posted on Facebook on this same day however many years ago. So that the harvest does not appear too meager, other people's posts in which we are mentioned by name are also displayed. The application Timehop functions similarly, by presenting earlier user comments and photos from diverse sources (Facebook, Twitter, Dropbox) for twenty-four hours, based on the same day a year before. To the extent that social networks have made the public realm a space for private things, it is only logical that applications like this should translate the concept "Today in History"—with which we are all familiar from television—to individual lives. But while on television the memorability of a news item is backed up by its coverage ten, twenty, or a random number of years before, here it is simply assumed, based on the passage of time.

At the same time, this enforced recollecting does not correspond at all to the recollection the madeleine inspires in Proust. The impulse comes from outside in Proust's case, too, but it merely activates a link that already exists in the unconscious of the remembering man, as something that is meaningful for him. If this were not the case, the madeleine would remain a small French pastry that is consumed without any sense that the person doing so is passing up an opportunity to remember. Precisely this option of meaninglessness does not exist for the memories served up by Timehop and Facebook. Here the occasion for recollection also signals a duty to recollect, and not remembering betrays a corresponding perceptible lack of capacity.

This incapacity, admittedly, is less a negative statement about the subject than a comment on the technology of automatized narration that precedes the notion of recollection: When photographs, comments, status updates, and other information about our activities on and beyond Facebook are more or less automatically and unconsciously deposited in the archive, it is hardly surprising if later on we cannot call them up in our memory. The temporal logic that is embodied in anniversaries may be an established means of both individual and collective remembrance, but in each case it is based on the presumption of an undoubted meaningfulness: birthday, graduation, marriage, establishment of a state, conclusion of a peace agreement ... With the anniversary logic of Timehop and Facebook, things become important without having proven their importance, like the gigantic ice cream sundae we had at the mall that time. The photo was semiconsciously transmitted to Facebook, spontaneously and routinely, while our thoughts were already halfway into the whipped cream. Now the image is back, as a representative of past life, as the hero of that day exactly five years ago.

ALIEN MEMORY

The result of this process is the production of memory under the sign of a meaningless logic of anniversaries.

Emphasized by its repetition, the shopping trip lives on in our mind without further technical assistance and is remembered again, in the future, because technical assistance once reminded us of it. The automatized reference to an anniversary multiplies the automatization that originally determined the creation of the entry. Automatized remembering is the end of forgetting, which after all is the precondition for every reasonable memory process. Thus, it devalues the emotional power of what is ultimately remembered. Memory is no longer a seismograph of one's own life, but the product of diverse technologies.

The more social variant of this other-directed remembering can be found in the response of the network, that is of the Facebook friends whose likes, shares, and comments basically codetermine the contents of our own Facebook page. The network is the second coauthor, along with the software that is working in the background. It can respond, in turn, to the software's memory offerings by applying likes and comments to entries that were made years ago and that the software is now re-collecting. Something that at the time already didn't mean anything further thus gets a chance to gain more recent emphasis, if it is ennobled by a sufficient number of likes. Thus my "friends" assign a specific value to the various signs of my past, a value that adheres to the signs and that henceforth determines my gaze at my own history. And who, among our friends, doesn't, in one way or another, love gigantic ice cream sundaes?

When we look at automatized memory through the lens of memory politics, we locate its deeper meaning in the equal rights that are afforded to all potential objects. The constellation of seemingly meaningless reports and recollections extends beyond culturally canonized events like school graduations, family gatherings, and vacation trips, and provides even ordinary things with access to the narrower circle of memory. The logic of photography, which, as the first great advocate of the banal, made it visible and memorable, is now applied to the photographs themselves, which are summoned for recollection irrespective of whether they have been witness to our marriage or to the shopping trip. If it is true that after our death we will be recognized by the things that were important to us, our posterity may be more than a little astonished to find this in our digital legacy, ahead of all other keepsakes: an ice cream sundae with chocolate sauce and whipped cream.

TECHNICAL INTROJECTION

With increasingly high levels of algorithmic performance, however, even automatic remembering could become meaningful. Let's imagine a time-leap app that calls up occasions for remembering based not on banal anniversary logic, but on correspondence with our actual situation. Just as Google's goal for the future is not to tell us what we should do next (say, something we haven't done for a year), but rather what (without already knowing it) we *want* to do next, the algorithmically skilled memory-prompts that we can expect to see in the future would likewise have to originate within us. The technical system would have to compute, from our present and past data, the specific recollection that is located close to a specific moment in time, and to call up the precise occasion for the memory that we ourselves would have generated if our neuronal system were still capable of doing so.

Concretely, in relation to the first example discussed here: the real-time purchase of a madeleine (after the abolition of the cash economy, the system will undoubtedly have access to this information) will call up an image from childhood in which our aunt (this information will also be present in the system of the future) dipped a madeleine in tea for us. The only problem: the memory should appear only after the madeleine comes into actual contact with the tea and our palate. But that can be resolved, too, once the teacup is connected to the Internet of things.

This closed circuit of technically generated recollections may be frightening. But who knows what we will think about it once we have arrived there? Humanity changes along with its technology. Who, nowadays, is disturbed by the fact that software reminds us who has a birthday when? How could I be opposed if, when reading a Rilke text online or watching a film, it reminded me of the friend who had once "liked" it?

The only certain thing is this: my lost friend remained longer than a day in Duino, Rilke's *Elegies* in his bag and the thought in his mind that "everything here," this "fleeting world," needs us, in order to find shelter from the ignorant attention of these times, "us, the most fleeting of all," shelter *in* us.

The haiku is like an everyday status update: *Spring breeze / The boatman / Chews his pipe*, to cite one example by Matsuo Bashō. Or another, by Kobayashi Issa: *In spring rain / A pretty girl / Yawning*. A brief, verbal increase in momentum, which Roland Barthes described as "the extinguishing of language in favor of a certainty of reality," the "absence of meaning, of interpretability."[1] The writer means no more than he says: The boatman, the yawning. Things are at rest in themselves. Situations are retained in their sheer existence, without context or deeper meaning. In the same vein, the 1689 travel diary *Oku no Hosomichi* by Bashō is an enumeration of unconnected events, each completely dedicated to the moment rather than subjugated to a narrative system.[2] Is haiku the secret model for Facebook?

TO SPEAK WORDLESSLY

On Facebook, you can only find haiku in disguise. They appear as photographs whose "noeme," as Barthes continues, is echoed by the "reality effect" of haiku with striking sobriety: "That's how it was."[3] This is precisely what most status updates on Facebook and other social networks amount to—photos of the moment that intend only to say: that's how it is right now.

The comparison falters because, as Barthes himself admits, "Photography is forced to *say* everything: about the boatman, what clothing he's wearing, his age, the filth." Haiku, in contrast, abbreviate their accounts to a few words. In this *less*, however, lies the *more* of observation and selection. Photography only "says" everything because it shows but doesn't tell. A haiku, on the other hand, "shows" what is important when it ignores the boatman's clothing but mentions his pipe.

In terms of perception, haiku is actually closer to painting than to photography, because the two former mention or show the butterfly in the park on a Sunday afternoon only if it is meaningful to the observer. The photographer, however, might retain it without even having noticed. The decisive difference is not between visual and linguistic representation, but rather between representation and recording. Recording is technical and therefore unconscious and objective, while representation is made by hand and therefore conscious and subjective. In 1927, Siegfried Kracauer described this difference as the shift from interpretation to documentation: "For in the artwork the meaning of the object takes on spatial appearance, whereas in photography the spatial appearance of an object is its meaning."[4] In other words, in photography, the butterfly prevails over the photographer, the object over the subject, accident over context.

STUNTED INSIGHT

Photography's epistemic paradox becomes clear when Kracauer points out its fragmentariness. Although or precisely because it shows everything, it is a fragment, since it "does not encompass the meaning" of what it shows. The adage describing this medial disposition has already been noted:

less is more. Painting or haiku is less and therefore says more about a situation than a photo that actually says nothing but shows everything.

For the same reason, Kracauer is ambivalent about what knowledge can be gained from photography. First, he concedes: "Never before has an age been so informed about itself, if being informed means having an image of objects that resembles them in a photographic sense." Second, he accuses photography of being a "means of organizing a strike against understanding,"[5] because objective portrayals of reality do not imply insight into it. The paradox is once again based on photography's specific form of expression that shows instead of describing.

Precisely because photography says nothing, it also withholds nothing. It may be blind to the butterfly, but it is therefore also impartial—just like Lady Justice, the person-ification of equity with her blindfold. Photography will always show the butterfly, even if it is munching its way through the fruit as a caterpillar. The haiku might leave it unmentioned in order not to disrupt the idyll of a summer's day: *The strawberries / on the plate / in the garden*. The "This is how it was" of the haiku is always just an assertion.

KNOWLEDGE GAINED

The good parts of photography can be had without the bad if showing follows telling, that is, by describing reality, which the photo shows in much more detail, in order to bring it into consciousness. I'm referring not to the division of labor, but rather to its sequence. If some people were to take photos and others describe them, the latter would have all of the insight. If things are to proceed democratically, everyone must do everything.

An alternative social network that not only abstains from capitalizing on private information, but also seeks to prevent itself from dumbing things down with the wrong type of media consumption, would allow people to post a photo only if they described it. And as a haiku at that, which would compel the writer to concentrate on the essential. Of course, the essential is a question of perspective, which is why counterhaiku would soon be put forward in the comments. The result could be a collection of haiku on the same image—a collective exercise in seeing and saying, a social game of a completely different quality than FarmVille or Mafia Wars.

At some point, this playful challenge would cause people to select photos based on their polyvalent haiku potential. The winning picture would prompt the most haiku, and so ever more complex, ambivalent photos would be posted. At some point, other visual media would be involved, and the selection of images alone would emphasize how far they go beyond mere showing. Vermeer's realistic image of a woman reading placed next to Georges Braque's cubist one, for example, would result in a riot of haiku.

The social network of the future would remediatize the Japanese genre of the *haiga*, a minimalistic drawing with a haiku that once united showing and telling. It overcomes the "indifference toward what the things mean," which Kracauer maligned in 1927 as the problem of "photographs by their sheer accumulation."[6]

Here is a photo that I recently would have liked to have taken: a woman in Hong Kong's bustling Times Square navigating her way through the crowd while reading. At first I thought she was looking at her phone, like most people here. Then I saw the book in her hand. I would have loved to take a photo of this surprising event. But I didn't have a smartphone with me, which is also probably why I noticed this episode at all.

It was like a scene in a film from long ago. However, anyone who isn't merely nostalgic for the protection of endangered media would inquire about the title of her book before they decided to prefer this woman over everyone weaving through the crowd with a smartphone in hand. After all, why should a pulp novel in the old medium be better than a newspaper culture section in the new one? Of course, we suspect that very few phones show the culture section. And who hasn't caught grown adults playing Candy Crush Saga on the subway? Adult fathers absorbed in Jelly Blast instead of playing with their children, or at least handing them the phone! Older women with an obsession for puzzle games who are nonetheless too young to pass for Brecht's "shameless old lady."

But the content isn't the point here. This isn't about the infantilization or dumbing down of society. It's about the medium itself and the ambient attention it allows us to wield in the world.

VISION IMPAIRMENT

One of Kafka's strangest statements goes: "We photograph things in order to drive them out of our minds."[1] A storage medium as a means of repression? Kafka takes note of a phenomenon that emerged with the availability of affordable cameras beginning in the late nineteenth century, and not just in the burgeoning tourism sector: the mechanical reproduction of reality without its recognition. As the Italian philosopher Giorgio Agamben put it in 1978, experience is delegated to recording media: "Standing face to face with one of the great wonders of the world (let us say the *patio de los leones* in the Alhambra), the overwhelming majority of people have no wish to experience it, preferring instead that the camera should."[2] The unbearable lightness of photography delegates seeing to the camera. Exceptions only confirm the rule: art students and tourists who poke around for days seeking subjects for their photos, until finally, with decisive precision, they take the two or three photos that matter.

The problem is older than the term *selfie*. And of course it also concerns the auratic proof of having been there: me at the Eiffel Tower, me with the *Mona Lisa*. This phenomenon, still occurring in the twenty-first century, is as nostalgic as letter writing. Must one really produce photographic evidence when GPS data exist that can identify our location and everything in our surroundings? But this question misses the real heart of the problem.

Kafka and Agamben didn't suspect that one day the digital camera would make taking photographs indiscriminate, and that the smartphone would make cameras omnipresent. Today, our phones contain cameras, and people say hello photographically with a Snapchat snapshot of whatever is going on at the moment. The two men's statements have come to pass with a radicality they couldn't have foreseen: we delegate whatever happens to us to the camera instead of consciously processing it ourselves. We take a photo instead of finding the words that would describe what we feel.

Kafka's contemporary Walter Benjamin provides the counterargument to his statement, extolling the knowledge gained through photography in the visual unconscious: that which otherwise is concealed during the course of an action becomes visible through its isolation and recording. A movement of the hand or a turn of the head suddenly becomes the starting point for a deeper understanding of what is really happening. However, this assumes that one spends more time looking at a photo than taking it. Less and less often is that the case.

Under the laws of the social media attention economy, photos aren't studied, just briefly apprehended, quickly liked, and clicked away forever. Some people manage to go through ten pictures between two floors on the elevator. Real observation looks different, and today perhaps it could be achieved only through an inverse-Snapchat mechanism: instead of making the photo visible for only ten seconds, you would have to wait for a whole minute before you could scroll to the next one. An alternative to this mechanical deceleration of reception would be the verbal transformation of the image: if one's own eyes spoke again instead of the camera, by turning the photo into words.

VERBAL PHOTOGRAPHY

"A nun, littering," "a doghouse with a snarling pitbull inside, beside a children's swingset," "a woman in fitness workout wear; running shoes, shorts, and an active top; standing by herself in a deserted aisle of a fluorescent-lit supermarket, her arms crossed in front of her chest, tears smearing her cheeks while she unwaveringly stared at the store's selection of baby diapers." Such texts are to be found on Michael David Murphy's blog, *Unphotographable.com*, under the slogan "This is a picture I did not take …"[3]

The inspiration for this "regression" in the history of media was a trip Murphy took to majority-Muslim Ethiopia, where photographing people, and especially women, is frowned upon. The amateur photographer returned with a newfound love of the old cultural techniques of describing, imagining, and fantasizing.

These texts vouch for nothing: not the messy nun, not the growling dog, not the weeping jogger, who is strongly reminiscent of Hemingway's famous six-word novel: "For sale: baby shoes, never worn." But whether what is presented has really been seen (in that way) is of secondary importance when what really matters is thinking of it. A written "copy" of a photo that never happened secures the lived as the experienced because it must pass through the mind. For example, you can show a photo of something without having seen it (the visual unconscious), but you cannot write something without having thought it. Every word secures the dominance of the viewer over his or her object; no butterflies enter the "picture" by accident. The verbal reproduction of reality attests to having been there, perhaps not authoritatively, but in a certain way more authentically than the obligatory photo for social media.

ALTERNATIVES

Should we proscribe the photo in social media and return to describing as an older cultural technique and a bastion against the ways in which the new blinds us? Maybe a yearly No Picture Day would be enough, similar to Buy Nothing Day, which takes place after Thanksgiving and has existed since 1992 as a protest against consumer culture, as well as No Internet Day, which falls on the first Friday in March. No Picture Day would be the day when cameras fall silent; a day of short texts instead of photos, written self-descriptions instead of selfies: a field day for teachers and educational policy makers. Individualized versions would be less dramatic, for example, if this day fell on each person's birthday, which would be technically easy to configure on social networks. A birthday is the perfect moment for contemplation, for looking back and forward, for a few lines of reflection instead of photos that are always the same but with different faces, different cakes, and a different number of candles.

Alternatively to No Photo Day, seeing and photographing can also be reconciled with social apps that allow us to delegate the latter in order to have time for the former. In summer 2015, Facebook released the Moments app, which allows you to gather other peoples' photos in which you yourself are tagged. The plausible explanation and advice is: stop taking the same photo ten times with ten different phones! This plea to the collective consciousness also sums up our era's answer to Kafka: by letting others photograph the moment in alternation, you can enjoy it yourself, free from distraction and in full presence of mind. It marks the return to the present under the sign of its mechanical reproduction, amended by automatic distribution.

The future of this app is its extension to moments that we experience without friends. One day, when everything in the world is photographed many times over, and our smartphones automatically, constantly, and precisely register our current GPS data, photos will appear on Facebook that others already have taken of what we've just seen. Undoubtedly, soon there will also be an app that inserts our portraits into these unknown photos: "me and the Eiffel Tower" as a collaboration.

9 THE DIALECTICS OF PARTICIPATION

Radio came too soon. The society that invented it was by no means sufficiently advanced for it, as Bertolt Brecht observed in a lecture he gave in 1932 on the function of radio: "The public was not waiting for the radio, but rather the radio was waiting for the public." Instead of handing everyone a microphone and bringing society into conversation with itself, Brecht said, people in broadcasting were imitating the old theatrical and print media, addressing the masses from the "stage" of the ether. Brecht thought that the task of turning radio from an "apparatus of distribution" into "the finest possible communications apparatus in public life" was impossible to achieve under the existing social order, but would be possible in another one, which it was therefore necessary to propagate.[1]

A medium as starting point for the overthrow of an entire social order? The idea isn't so outlandish if we consider the social consequences of the invention of printing. But it would take until the end of the twentieth century before everyone would have access to a microphone. Only with the Internet and then, in earnest, with the social networks of the web 2.0 was there a bidirectional medium that allowed every message recipient to become a sender. Did that mean that the public Brecht had envisioned for radio was at hand?

DISCOURSE CULTURE

This time the medium came too late, although at first people thought its arrival was just in time. The coincidental demise of socialist social systems in the same year as the birth of the World Wide Web seemed to argue for removing all socially utopian ambitions to the realm of new media. So it was no surprise when, shortly thereafter, the independence of cyberspace from real-world governments was declared—an idea that admittedly lasted only as long, as hardly anyone was genuinely interested in occupying this space.[2] Today, all the energies of social change are produced and consumed there, under slogans like "big data," "industry 4.0," and the "Internet of things."

For a time, the optimism outlived even the commercial capture that accompanied the new millennium, and it still survives today among some very stubborn types. For the Internet, as cyberspace is now more matter-of-factly known, continues to be a space that is freely accessible: There are no more gatekeepers, no thought police, no elite opinion-makers, but instead free access to information and a much-expanded public realm. Admittedly, the often-invoked comparison with Jürgen Habermas's historical study, *The Structural Transformation of the Public Sphere*, was always already limping, since he himself held that even the model of deliberative democracy was better off in the asymmetrical, ideally also self-reflective and multiperspectival discourse culture of the traditional mass media than in the symmetrical and decentralized culture of the Internet. For the Internet not only frees public discussion from institutional control, it also frees it from the central role of political themes and creates a public that is doubly dispersed: a public that is broken down into very small groups, which are scarcely willing to consider anything that exceeds the compass of their smartphones.[3]

The "communication apparatus in public life," which for Brecht and numerous others after him promised the emancipation of the individual, undermines—such is the bitter irony of its success—the minimal demand that Brecht posed for radio: that as the locus of political information and discussion it should sharpen society's critical awareness. Brecht's critique of the radio—that "a technical invention with such a natural aptitude for decisive public functions is met by such anxious efforts to maintain *without consequences* the most harmless entertainment possible"—still applies, indeed more emphatically, to the Internet—this despite WikiLeaks, political bloggers, and the critical commentary that bravely persists here and there.[4]

CULTURE INDUSTRY 2.0

The "organization of the excluded," with which radio was supposed to confront the "powers that exclude," has become reality in diverse social networks, but not in order to challenge the status quo, as Brecht and others once hoped.[5] The end of history that was proclaimed in 1989 also spelled the end of Adorno's perspective, according to which history—as the emergence of an emancipated, exploitation-free life—had not yet begun. Talk of a life freed from social delusion (*Verblendungszusammenhang*) has faded away. Amusement is no longer disdained as a compromise with false life, and emancipation is now primarily taken to mean self-expression and branding on the social network.

The survival trick of the society Brecht and Adorno wanted to do away with is participation. It starts economically, with the transformation of society's members into small-scale investors, and continues as a media phenomenon that makes the culture of participation a hot commodity in the advertising industry. Corporate sponsorship is the great hope of "Generation Like," which is doing everything it possibly can to become famous on Twitter, YouTube, and Instagram. After being successfully "discovered," the fortunate individual then consistently wears only certain sneakers, T-shirts, and baseball caps in her skateboard videos, or drives repeatedly through the video clip in a blue Ford Fiesta.[6]

Thus, teenagers become advertising partners and occasionally even sponsors themselves, if their links and shared performances draw attention to other YouTubers. This solidarity of the formerly excluded, and even the self-marketing, would certainly have earned the approbation of Brecht, and maybe Adorno as well, if the heroes of the social media were ultimately using their newfound power as the lords and masters over millions of pairs of eyes and ears to spread the really important messages among the people.

But accidental revolutionaries are as rare as political memes. For Generation Like, the end justifies the means even where no liberty, equality, or fraternity is involved. This generation has an astonishing confidence in its self-marketing, and has no problem boasting, as a sign of growing success, that it has attracted the interest of Taco Bell or McDonalds. The name "Generation Like" refers not only to the "likes" it is so eager to garner, but also to its good relations with society in general. Its vocabulary is appropriately positive: to this generation, "opportunism" means seizing opportunities, and "selling out" means that all the tickets for an event have already been purchased.

The Internet came too late for what it could possibly have become. After the free market economy, with its tangible consumer culture, had won out over competing contenders for the future of humankind, the new media system could not expect much more from people than what they had made it into: a virtual shopping center that is accessible at all times and places, with a few niches consigned to social creativity and political education, which, surrounded by advertising and subject to the laws of the attention economy, ultimately serve as supply chains for the neoliberal social model. And, what's worse, the new medium even sucks in all the older media too.

INFOTAINMENT

Classical journalism has suffered for some time from the fact that more and more people are getting their information from social networks, but until recently at least the links readers encountered on the networks' sites steered them to journalism's own sovereign territory, where journalistic responsibility had a seat at the table and it was even possible to give covert nourishment to less popular but actually important news items. With "Instant Article," Facebook's latest star attraction, the last defense of *zoon politikon* is being dismantled, in the name of democracy.

Officially, as always, the change is about improving communication, this time even political communication. People don't want to wait very long for a news article to load, and as a result many of them don't even bother to click on the link. Hence Mark Zuckerberg's response to a journalist's question, at an in-house virtual press conference on July 1, 2015, about Facebook's plans to support "good journalism." Zuckerberg's solution: embed the news items on Facebook's server, so they can load in less than three hundred milliseconds, instead of three seconds or more, as in the past.

What many people might regard as a coup is for Zuckerberg merely part of his educational mission: "When news is as fast as everything else on Facebook, people will naturally read a lot more news. That will be good for helping people be more informed about the world, and it will be good for the news ecosystem because it will deliver more traffic."[7] Interestingly, "news," here, evidently refers to stories filed by members of the Fourth Estate, which Facebook's "news feed" had effectively and successfully depoliticized as early as 2010. But this is absolutely no grounds for hope.

The rationale offered for Zuckerberg's plan to preserve quality journalism is simultaneously its death sentence. For how much intellectual attention can a news article claim, if three seconds is already too long to wait for it to appear? Quickly downloaded also means quickly consumed, between exciting status updates. The rule of thumb of the attention economy is a simple one: the easier it is to like something, the more likes it gets. The essay on *Kulturkampf* will face a tough road if it is competing with the eyewitness account of the double murder in the Rue Morgue. Picking the winner requires no explanation; it materializes in a form that is fully consonant with grassroots democracy: by the numbers. Verbal comments, if there are any, don't carry much weight, and while it may be important to the editor in chief that ten people wrote eloquently formulated, enthusiastic comments on the *Kulturkampf* story, the shareholders will not be impressed.

This may sound cynical, but it actually entails a subtle and far-reaching critique. Social networks place a radical bet on public opinion polling; they completely disempower all the experts who think they know better when it comes to what people actually need or ought to want. For Zuckerberg, education for social maturity begins with getting rid of waiting and ends with a discussion-free plebiscite of likes. And because he wants to give people what they want, he says in the same interview that he sees the future of journalism in "rich content," such as videos (instead of "just text and photos"), and in "immersive content like VR." In 2014, in anticipation of this development, Facebook spent $2 billion on the Oculus Rift VR headset company. In 2016, it invented Facebook Live as a video livestreaming experience for everyone and everything.

SELF-DEFEATING SUCCESS

Of course it is true: Facebook's social model aims, to the maximum extent possible, to corral its users within its own sphere of influence, since this is what generates the data and attention that it is then able to sell. Fears about Facebook as a media monopoly and Zuckerberg as uber-censor are justified, as are complaints about the media's financial dependence on advertising revenues, which now forces many news outlets into a kind of horse-trading with Facebook. The real problem, however, is neither Zuckerberg nor commerce, but the Internet itself.

The Internet would not have come at the right time earlier, either. Its dispositives—hyper-reading, multitasking, power browsing, filter bubble, instant gratification, quantification, and so on—are diametrically opposed to the public sphere that Brecht intended. With the next distraction only a click away, patience for anything that requires effort evaporates. Anyone who doesn't have quick responses to complex questions is promptly and publicly punished by a withdrawal of likes. So is the medium responsible? Is it the human condition as such? Is the anthropological and technological constellation an overlay over political and economic interests in the background?

Whatever the answer turns out to be, one thing is clear. If, in the future, the journalists 'stories—embedded in Facebook's news feed along with the videos of Facebook friends (which, unlike the journalists, will show the victims lying in pools of their own blood)—have to compete for likes, a process that began as hope will end, in an unanticipated way:

the "organization of the excluded" materializes as a communication culture in which, as Zuckerberg argued when he introduced the news feed, "a squirrel dying in front of your house may be more relevant to your interests right now than people dying in Africa."[8] Liberation, once again, flips back into dependency, this time as a dialectics of participation.

Brecht's contemporaries already saw the first signs of this reversal in the 1920s, when they warned not only about "radiotitis," excessive radio-listening, but also about "tunitis," the constant tuning of the dial from one station to another. The variable tuner was the beginning of the end of the radio as a people's university and apparatus of emancipation, for it made it possible to keep dashing off to wherever something more interesting was going on. No one could have envisioned the temptations offered by its technological successors—the zapping of the remote or the clicking through of hyperlinks. But the criticism of the radio audience shows that already in Brecht's era not everyone was waiting in anticipation for the public sphere that radio was beginning to create.[9]

Fear came early. It arrived when the Internet became popular, and those who were already coming and going there asked themselves how to organize this deluge of information from everyone and everywhere. There were lists of links on websites and in newspapers, and there were even printed brochures with web addresses to provide a bit of clarity. The irony of this form of presentation is unmistakable, but it is not the only paradox to speak of. These lists of links on paper or online were recommendations from experts and the new know-it-alls who wanted to tame the new in an old way: with judgment.

Today it's hard to imagine, but back then Yahoo had two dozen employees who carefully looked over each website. The information was arranged in a hierarchy determined by the offline world. Thus the website of the Messianic Jewish Alliance of America was placed in the category "Judaism," which was part of the category "Religion," which in turn was part of the category "Society and Culture." It was an attempt to address the complexity of the digital world using the classification methods of the analog world. And it brought all of the problems of such a method along with it—for example, the protests of "real" Jews against the inclusion of the Messianic Jewish Alliance of America. Most Messianic Jews were born to a Jewish mother, but they believe in Jesus.

That makes them a heretical sect in the eyes of many, one that doesn't fit in the category of Judaism, or rather shouldn't be found in it, and in any case shouldn't be listed there by Yahoo, so the complaints went.

Then came Google and the end of the hierarchy. You no longer rifled through cabinet A, drawer B, file C to find something; you simply entered the search term. The old ontological model of organization was replaced by the relational database, which could assign the Messianic Jewish Alliance of America the tag "Jewish" as well as "heretical" and let the public decide. It was the transition from the order of experts to the referendum of the masses, which determined the characterization of a website based on its links and tags, dictating its popularity and its visibility along with it: the more people link to a site, the more important it is, according to Google's simple but multibillion-dollar-winning idea.

This switch from qualitative to quantitative assessment was based on one final qualitative decision: that quantity is the more reliable criterion. Numbers, according to the solution of the hour, say more than a thousand words. It didn't matter what anyone thought about an idea or a person, only if they were popular. That's how it is with every vote whose winners are determined by a count. It's a deeply democratic process. That's precisely the point: the switch from Yahoo to Google wasn't just a transition of power in the online search-engine market segment. It also wasn't just a technological paradigm shift. It was a political revolution that replaced the judgment of a few with the power of the masses, expertocracy with numerocracy.

COLLECTIVE INTELLIGENCE

Long before the term "wisdom of the crowd" became popular, there was a book with the title *Collective Intelligence.* Its author, the French philosopher Pierre Lévy, would later describe the Internet as a knowledge community that extended beyond all borders, and as "universality without totality."[1] The Internet is antitotalitarian because content can no longer control its environment. Instead, everything is connected to everything, and must prove itself in relation to the other with messages, comments, and observations. Lévy viewed this as an expansion of the project of the Enlightenment. At least as far as Wikipedia is concerned, he proved to be correct.

But the masses can also be wise when they vote, not just when they discuss something. On a fall day in 1906, the British polymath Francis Galton proved this when he had eight hundred visitors at an agricultural exhibition guess the weight of an ox. Of course, there were many wrong guesses, but since they overshot in both directions (sometimes too little, sometimes too much), the errors evened each other out, and taken together, they ultimately led to an average that was only one pound over the correct number. It was a moment of glory for the wisdom of the crowd, but also for democracy. As Galton later wrote about the experiment, the average participant in this estimate was as well prepared for it as the average voter is prepared to assess political issues. If the crowd reliably hit on the weight of the ox, according to Galton's logical conclusion, their judgment in democratic decisions was also to be trusted.[2]

Galton was more confident about the matter in 1906 than Nicolas de Condorcet over a century before him. In his jury theorem, Condorcet emphasized that the odds of getting a correct answer to a yes or no questions from a group increases along with the size of the group, and that the impartiality of laypeople is even a benefit—which, I would note, also ultimately defines the concept of trial by jury. However, when faced with the masses' lack of education and voting competence, he preferred representative democracy to direct democracy, so that the power remains with those who know what they're talking about based on reflection and discussion, and what they must consider when making their decision.

This demand for enlightened voting competence seems to have been diminished by the Internet, since the world can be reduced to whatever seems personally obvious to us based on algorithms' filters and our own preferences. The most recent answer to the plethora of information in the information age ensnares people in a "me-loop" of auto-propaganda. Contrary to what Galton and Condorcet surmise, the result is the *folly* of the crowd: a majority of like-minded people mutually affirming and encouraging each other, instead of balancing their opinions with numerous others.[3]

GATEKEEPERS

The Internet means a changing of the gatekeepers. Before, experts, administrators, and what Michel Foucault called the "discourse police" determined who could communicate what in public, but since the advent of the Internet you no longer need the approval of an editor, publisher, or organizer. What's needed now is attention, which generally used to be assured as soon as you passed the gatekeepers. At the same time, this entails a change in the way success is measured. Before, you were already successful if you had access to the public space because it meant you had passed the experts' test. Now the only test is that of public reception. In the currency of social networks, the power of the superior argument is assumed based on the higher number of likes; quality equals quantity.

The criteria for assessment in the digital meritocracy is not subject-specific, but rather based on the attention economy. Whatever you do, however good or bad it is, its success is based on views, shares, likes, followers, and retweets. As we know from popularity-driven websites like Reddit and Digg, the deepest content is rarely to be found under the highest number. "Social bookmarking" (the specialist term for recommendation lists created by Internet users) robs the logic of rating of its last opposition, which editors, directors, publishers, and other traditional gatekeepers still voice based on professional ethic. The much-touted wisdom of crowds degenerates into the power of the many, who push articles on Kim Kardashian or cute dogs to the top of the "must read/see" list. But that isn't the only problem with the change of gatekeepers. The paradox lies in the fact that being measurable doesn't prevent the system from being manipulated.

This is the case when invisible editors in the backrooms of platforms "correct" the results of social bookmarking.

This secret return of the experts caused a stir—and rightly so—in May 2016 in reaction to Facebook's manipulation of its statistical trend notifications. It was an instance of plying the old principle in the garb of the new, except this time without the rules and proof of qualifications that the old system brought with it. The discourse police had been privatized in a sense, and as a secret rapid deployment force, they answered only to the owners of the platform: the monopoly on state force had been transferred to the head of Facebook.

In this case, the statistics were manipulated after the fact by human intervention, but before that they had already been distorted by the conditions of communication that produce the data. Given the short time that young people today spend on the rapidly turning communication carousel, they often like a video report or newspaper article that already has many likes. Some of them will look briefly at the video or article to be sure. But most of them trust blindly in the fact that quantity means quality. Likes breed likes, as Karl Marx would have said, had he written his *Capital* under the influence of the attention economy.

NUMERIC POPULISM

The phenomenon of numeric populism is older than the Internet. *Quantification* is the magic word in any form of administration, and it has always rendered experts unnecessary. Under the banner of numbers, even the clueless can reach a decision, because everyone knows that five is more than four. It's well known that important political discussions have already fallen victim to entertaining talk shows through the logic of the ratings, as is the fact that politicians base their statements on survey results. Numerical superiority always gave the masses dominance over the old gatekeepers. But this feedback loop isn't the only factor, and certainly not the most absurd aspect of numeric populism.

Quantifiability has also become the basis for assessment in universities. Therefore, standardized tests and grade-point averages for students have been introduced, income scales for graduates, citation indexes, impact factors, and seminar evaluation statistics, as well as ranking lists for universities. The craze for scoring and ranking aims at accountability through accounting, allowing even freshly minted administrative assistants to make statements about the reputations and professional success of veteran professors in their department. With the digitization of society and the cult of the interaction paradigm, this accounting model has now extended to all possible domains. Not even art curation has been spared.

At the end of 2014, the *Wall Street Journal* published an article titled "When the Art Is Watching You." The lead image showed sculptures of torsos with cameras for heads.[4] German literary scholars will be immediately reminded of Rainer Maria Rilke's famous poem "Archaic Torso of Apollo" (1908) when they think of artists gazing expectantly out of their works (in Rilke's case a headless statue) at observers. The well-known closing verse has given generations of literature students goosebumps: "for here there is no place /

that does not see you. You must change your life."[5] But the article isn't about Rilke's poem, or at least it's about the poem only insofar as the modern, technical eye inverts his conclusion into its complete opposite.

The audience isn't being watched by the art, but rather by the mediators of art, the data analysts who evaluate the public's behavior: how often do they come to the museum, to which exhibitions, how long do they stand in front of which works of art, what do they buy in the museum shop? Then the tech people show the curators and art educators diagrams and tables to demonstrate which topics will ensure more visitors. And so in this case, ratings also rule in favor of the economy. The question is no longer "What is meaningful in the history of art?" but rather "What's trending?" It is the death of experts at the very center of high culture.

THE AESTHETICS OF EXPERTLESSNESS

As is so often the case, what became a societal problem through the Internet had its beginnings in art. Loss of privacy, for example, is an idea that began with the avant-garde, who conceived of transparency as an attack on bourgeois culture, which was still the case for self-surveillance projects in the Internet's pioneering days. Similarly, the death of experts was also proclaimed in art as the death of the artist, which some artists began to press for in the 1960s under the names of chance, behaviorist, and participatory art. These "suicide theorists" demanded that the artist be less involved in the production of art, promoting a corresponding relocation of power from the artist to the audience.[6]

One example of this transfer of power were interactive installations, which reacted to the audience's behavior—that is, the audience "completed" (as it was grandiosely termed) the installation. Another is participatory art with a focus on cultural activism, which since the end of the twentieth century has aimed to generate more open social situations. Dialogue and respect are the central tenets of this art form, an empathetic identification with the other rather than an "arrogant" appeal to change your life. It no longer employs the shock with which the Dadaists and many other artists alienated audiences; this is a group cuddle session. Art critics are inevitably included in the cuddling, since, if the goal is to free art from aesthetic or pedagogical objectives of "know-it-all" artists, there can hardly be positions from which to evaluate works of art. Instead, the measure of success is how many people participate, which ultimately makes the art inherently numerocratic.[7]

The death of experts ultimately occurs at the expense of those who are supposed to benefit from it. That becomes evident first and foremost in the realm of art, which serves the public by challenging it, unsettling it, making demands on it, and thus pushing the observers to move beyond themselves—as Adorno would later translate Rilke's verse. But if art is made to please people, it deprives them of the opportunity to ever be more than they already are. Adorno recognized this deception in the culture industry; now it is the unavoidable side effect of the death of experts, which is generally the effect of the Internet.

If we are no longer pestered by experiences that challenge us, and if we always have the option to choose what's fun now, we will never experience what a joy it can be to comprehend complex ideas and even be able to produce them ourselves. As in sports, the endorphins can't be had without effort and perseverance. But these virtues are dying in the culture of immediate gratification. Who has the patience anymore for something that isn't immediately comprehensible? In such cases, who thinks anymore that the problem lies with themselves? Along with the experts, we've also gotten rid of the *aspiration* that they brought to their audiences. There are no longer "chaperons" who admonish people to see things through or try a change of course: this is cowardice disguised as democracy.

The shitstorm *avant la lettre* was a literal one: in the Middle Ages, when delinquents were placed in the pillory, their fellow citizens frequently allowed little children to shower them with filth. When the term was invented later (in 1948, in Norman Mailer's World War II novel *The Naked and the Dead*), it had less to do with actual excrement than with the phrase "when the shit hits the fan." It was used in reference to a life-threatening combat situation or to generally risky prospects.

In its current German usage to refer to Internet phenomena the term has lost all scatological implications, even in metaphorical terms. Semantically, it is more of a "protest storm" than a "smear campaign." It in no way discredits those responsible for the storm, nor does its target receive automatic victim status. According to German linguists in 2011, a *shitstorm* is nothing more than an "unforeseen, ongoing wave of indignation on social networks and blogs about the behavior of public figures or institutions."[1]

Among the term's peculiarities is that it was named "Anglicism of the Year" in Germany, though it doesn't mean the same thing in German as it does in English. The supposed loan-word is a German neologism disguised as an English word. Just as surprising is the fact that Germans use such a foul-sounding word for something that is basically good. The indignation expressed is often the justified result of misconduct by those in power, who cannot be disciplined in any other way.

THE POWER OF THE CUSTOMERS

Let's take Vodafone as an example: on July 25, 2012, Corinna Julius posted a complaint on Vodafone's Facebook page titled "As soon as my contract runs out, I'm canceling everything!" about excessive direct debit charges for her smartphone contracts and terrible customer service. Instead of providing Corinna with the itemized call record she had requested, Vodafone "wanted to accommodate her" by waiving 250 euros of her fees, which prompted her to call Vodafone's dealings with its customers "a disgrace." "HELLO? Are you serious? I'm not paying the remainder of something that isn't even mine to begin with!!"[2]

Corinna's bad experience wasn't an isolated one, as the many comments that immediately showed up on Vodafone's Facebook page demonstrated. Complaints plus collective experience is the shitstorm's biotope. Vodafone reacted quickly but wrongly when it pointed Corinna to a contact form. Someone commented on July 31: "the fact that they still don't get that in cases like this you dont want to hear some empty standard phrase. and then they go show the whole world how they dont give a shit about problems like this. awesome vodafone! top notch!" The comment is titled "Shitstorming!" which isn't a slogan, but an exultant proclamation. After all, in the meantime Corinna's post had around 6,000 comments and 60,000 likes, three times as many as are required to reach critical shitstorm mass.

No way! says the web 2.0 world: Not on our watch! What once would have remained isolated frustration in the hearts of thousands now converges into a single outcry. Corinna certainly didn't intend to fuel the indignation, nor did she do anything to stoke it. But the matter wasn't in her hands anymore. The masses, which every large company wants to have as customers, are simultaneously a larger risk factor since online networks and customer websites have given individuals means of communication and a place to congregate. Anyone who doesn't invest in customer service, especially on their own website, will be forced to face the painful conclusion that social media isn't only good for viral marketing.

GUILTY BY ASSOCIATION

But you can't always do something about it yourself. Take Adidas as an example: On November 3, 2011, the German public broadcaster ARD ran an episode of the program *Brisant*, with a segment about the killing of stray dogs in Ukraine that might interfere with the Euros—the UEFA European Soccer Championship being held there. Admittedly, *Brisant* wasn't so much addressing Ukrainian communities as the European Soccer Association: "Killing dogs for the sake of soccer—that's not good publicity."[3] Within two days, a video of the segment was watched nearly 150,000 times on YouTube. "Euros 2012 on bloody sod"— This historically loaded sentence[4] stood at the top of

Berlin-resident Julia Akra's blog, which went online on November 9. One day later, the Austrian Michael Hillinger founded the Facebook group Stop Killing Dogs-euro 2012 in Ukraine. Now all that was needed were more words to fuel the fire.

By November 20, Michael's Facebook group had 30,000 fans (by the end of the month, it was 80,000), and Julia wrote, again without aversion to historical comparisons: "Let's go! Copy/paste to protest the dog Holocaust." Next came a list with the Facebook pages of Euros sponsors who could receive complaints. The dramatization (bloody sod, Holocaust) went hand in hand with the new addressees of the protest, which had already been suggested by the *Brisant* staff. One no longer addresses the Ukrainian government as citizens of Germany or Austria, since they pay little attention to international protest, as the Tymoshenko case demonstrated. Nor does one address the UEFA, the organizer of the Euros, which would be the most politically effective action. No, one speaks as a consumer and addresses international corporations whose responsibility may be questionable, but whose concern for the good reputation of their global brands is not.

Thus, Adidas, one of the Euros sponsors, became a target. "Dear sponsors of the Euros," wrote one shitstormer. "Do you know who I am? I'm a CONSUMER ... I can't change anything about what happens in Ukraine. But I'll promise you sponsors something: I'll stop watching the Euros on TV. I'll go without new ADIDAS jogging shoes ..."[5] Adidas saw many of the enraged comments on their website as spam and made the mistake of deleting them. Besides, Adidas wasn't killing any dogs! And if dogcatchers wear Adidas, that's not Adidas's fault! However, deleting the comments added fuel to the shitstorm fire because for social media activists, it amounted to brutal censorship. From this point on, it wasn't just the lives of dogs that were at stake, but also the pride of the net community. "Shitstorm over Blood-storm: The Power of Facebook" was the title of Julia's blog post the next day about the "online eraser" Adidas used to try "to keep its Facebook page as white as its jerseys." But "blood is hard to wash out—online or offline."[6]

The Ukrainian stray dogs became more and more dangerous for Adidas. It took them two days to respond, and even then they didn't make a clear commitment: "The Adidas Group is strongly opposed to all forms of cruelty to animals and expects the Ukrainian government to diligently pursue these accusations and take the appropriate action. We are watching this matter very closely and will continue to do so."[7] A general statement against killing dogs really isn't enough once the shitstorm has begun. It's a good thing that by the next day, Adidas could proclaim: "The UEFA has been in constant contact with the Ukrainian authorities, who have now promised to stop the killing of dogs immediately, and to legally prohibit it. We hope that the implementation will be immediate and effective!"

With that, the demand that Adidas withdraw as a sponsor of the Euros was rendered obsolete. The shitstorm died down after it had accomplished something: the topic was on the front page of German newspapers, and it was the lead headline on Spiegel Online for two days. Many national soccer players supported the campaign, and Nina Hagen even canceled a concert in Ukraine.[8] But the boycott of Adidas products never became a reality; it had been under discussion when the conversation shifted from Ukrainian dogs to the Asian children who work for Adidas. By changing the topic from one skeleton in the closet to another, certain politically motivated shitstormers attempted to turn the animal-lovers into class-warriors. To no avail, as quickly became evident.

SHITSTORMERS

Shitstorms feed on the opinionated nature of web 2.0 users, as well as on the logic of communication in new media. The website bearing the names of the guilty parties and providing an address for protest emails, the simplicity of copy-paste, the links to the center of other storms, and the tried-and-tested tools for emotionalization that mobilizes (videos of dogs in mass graves and poisoned dogs in the throes of death), search engines that find fuel for the shitstorm online in seconds, smartphones that make the storm mobile and uninterrupted—all of this means that in the critical phase of a shitstorm, likes accumulate at an average of 7 per minute, along with 0.7 comments, creating a flood of notifications that are overwhelming in the moment. If nothing else, the shitstorm thrives on communication overload.

For example, who wants to read all 6,000 comments produced by the Vodafone shitstorm in five days? Even Corinna couldn't do it, and so she overlooked Vodafone's answer at first, which was provided within an hour—and was buried in the other 670 comments that Corinna received in that first hour. Since Vodafone seemed to still owe Corinna and the other commenters an answer, people continued to pillory them. And so Vodafone was ironically doomed by something it really couldn't do anything about: the communication conditions of the competing media, where people write faster than they read.

Shitstorms thrive on rapid likes and goading comments, which fall into three categories: those written by followers, those by do-gooders, and those by trolls. Followers write one- or two-word comments in agreement, lending weight to what's been said without adding anything new. Do-gooders are new-media missionaries who want to advance, by whatever means necessary, the culture of transparency that they experience on Facebook and other social media every day. They expect everyone to explain everything and get extremely upset at old-fashioned claims such as "That's no business of yours." Trade secrets are no longer allowed in web 2.0, not even for private individuals.

Trolls are the people who post provocative, insulting comments instead of stopping at germane arguments. Though they don't care about truth or justice, they help to develop the shitstorm, which would quickly perish of its own redundancy without their comments. Provocative comments shake people awake, give them a scare, call for further reaction—from do-gooders and from other trolls. It keeps the communication active and increases the number of likes and posts, until the storm makes it into the classic media, which is its secret goal. In a certain sense, trolls are the shitstorm-system's autopoetic ruse, the entertaining answer to the devaluation of information. They're the soul of the storm in spite of themselves, since they're really only in it for the fun—and to convert any attention gained into more views for their own websites' Google AdSense advertising.

FLASH-MOB POLITICS AND EXTRA-PARLIAMEN-TARY OPPOSITION

The guilt by association that Adidas bore as a sponsor may seem unfair, but only at first glance. If we take a closer look at the situation, the redirection of the protest seems to be a logical consequence of the "triumph of post-democracy," which has increasingly shifted power away from democratically legitimated authorities and toward interest groups and the economic elite.[9] In a sense, the shitstorm is the Internet's answer to the neoliberal extortion of the state by large globally active corporations, which pose publicly as purely economic units but have long acted covertly as political decision makers. As was made clear by the discussion of taxation in the context of the Panama Papers, you can't drain a swamp if the frogs are all members of the planning commission. The shitstorm is the expression of the power of the people in an age when it can assemble digitally: a Fifth Estate that doesn't accept the concept of "too big to fail."

The infrastructure of the new protest culture was created by those under attack. Their social media presence offers a staging ground for the grievances. These twenty-first-century protests may "only" happen in cyberspace instead of on the street, but they take place precisely on their targets' virtual premises. A new sort of extra-parliamentary opposition organizes as a flash mob, overrunning the customers and fans already present on a company's website. The shitstorm is the street riot of the Internet age, but without stones, truncheons, or injuries. It is the slactivist's preferred form of protest, which nonetheless offers more opportunity for citizen participation than online petitions and liking things—a sort of happening or public event whose length and outcome is determined by the public itself.

The shitstorm symbolizes the democratization of web 2.0 communication, in its problematic fashion. As opinionated and as grassroots democratic as this form of protest may be, the formation of its political will is not based on argumentation, but rather on emotionalization and dramatization. It is the shitstormers' gut instincts that become a political power here. This instinct stands in the way of discursive formation of judgment just as the dramatizing and personalization of politics do in our media society. Twenty-first-century extra-parliamentary opposition is no better than its elected representatives.

WHATEVER THE CROWD DESIRES

The shitstorm is more than the last form of protest available to the masses against the ruling elites. It is also the expression of mass society in the Internet age. For most shitstormers, the real motivation for their engagement isn't political at all; it's psychological, because, as a sort of self-lobbying on the part of the little person, it promises an intense—if brief and mediated—feeling of emotional security.

The modern individual's fear of contact with other people—so goes the psychological point of Elias Canetti's *Crowds and Power*—can be overcome only at the moment of fraternization with the "enemy"; in the ecstatic, blind embrace of the other in its multiplicity. The feeling of community, which the modern person lost long ago (unless they live in a nationalistic dictatorship), briefly flares again in this intoxication. This feeling of community is without structure because we do not know the people we are embracing—according to the central thesis of David Riesman's *The Lonely Crowd* (1950). But precisely therein lies the romantic glorification of this all-around fraternization: it overcomes all social, political, cultural, and religious differences that otherwise divide society by ignoring everything that makes individuals more than random representatives of the human species. In this respect, the individual aspect results from being a member of a group of strangers, which constitutes itself by separating from other strangers. Examples of this phenomenon include with increasing intensity music festivals, the Hajj and Pentecost celebrations, and political demonstrations, pogroms, genocides, and other xenophobic excesses.

The community of shitstormers is closer to a riot than to a demonstration, because they take shared views as the basis for action without any real discussion or voting. Like the Occupy movement and many other political protests today, it is horizontally organized. Many industrious bloggers and provocative trolls take the place of charismatic speakers and clear leadership. You can agree with Canetti by labeling this lynch-mob-like community a "baiting crowd," which can be understood as the modern version of the earlier "hunting pack": people gather in order to bring down a big animal together.

However, the purpose of the hunt is no longer to quell hunger, but rather to survive, which can be felt most intensely when the other is in the throes of death, as Lucretius realized more than two thousand years ago: "It is sweet to witness from the distant shore the distress of the other in the raging winds on the high-surging seas." In the shitstorm, this "shipwreck with spectator"[10] becomes a result, a targeted action, and the erstwhile witnesses of the accident become its cause. One's own feeling of power no longer results from observing the powerlessness of the other against the forces of nature, but rather by occupying the position of these forces oneself. Insofar as this feeling of power masks one's own sorrows in life, the baiting crowd (or hunting pack) is ultimately a sort of self-help group—a self-help group that operates under the conditions of digital media: participants remain anonymous, come together only temporarily, and embrace each other across the safe distance of the digital interface.

SHITSTORMER SHITSTORM

The psychoanalytic interpretation of the shitstorm explains why it is often directed against individuals and without the symbolic political value of improving the world that it would have if it were directed against the powerful. It often focuses on women who flirt with the wrong men, professors who say something wrong in their lecture, on all sorts of supposed social misbehavior and political incorrectness. The shitstorm then occurs under the auspices of the "good citizen" who places delinquents in the pillory without mercy or self-doubt, and who also doesn't mind hacking and publishing the delinquents' personal data (address, grade-point average, photos, photos of friends, etc.)—a process that the social network Hong Kong Golden (which, as a group of awkward nerds isn't safe from attacks itself) self-righteously calls "exposure culture."[11]

Such shitstorms often deserve a shitstorm of their own, because they misuse an important instrument of political resistance for personal dogmatism and selfish feelings of power, and in the long term they lead to a culture of self-censorship far beyond political correctness—to say nothing of the Saint Petersburg troll factories, where poor students harass opponents of the regime and civil rights advocates for money (and often against their own beliefs).[12]

Such a shitstorm for shitstormers was portrayed in 2016 in episode 6 of the third season of *Black Mirror*, "Hated in the Nation." The story takes place in a not-so-distant future, when critical journalists and tough rappers are attacked online with the hashtag #DeathTo, while millions of autonomous drone insects (ADIs) have taken over the pollination work of extinct bees. These ADIs are important to the plot because, like all artificial intelligence, they can be hacked, and because, as was to be expected, they are simultaneously being used by the state secret service as surveillance cameras with face-recognition software. They've turned them into drones, which hackers can send unerringly and inescapably to pursue the people at the top of the #DeathTo list. The death hashtag ultimately proves to be a parlor game that allows enraged citizens to move their favorite target to the top of the list with the appropriate posts, a "game with consequences," as it's succinctly called, because every day at five on the dot, an ADI burrows into the brain of the "winner" via their nose or ear. A game with deadlier consequences than expected, as it turns out: the three victims of the shitstorm were just decoys for punishing the baiting crowd, whose names and photos were ultimately loaded into the ADIs' central computer. As the show demonstrates with a finale à la Hitchcock's *The Birds*, the programmed angels of death cannot be escaped: 387,036 shitstormers die of ADI penetration—a merciless judgment upon a hunting pack that mercilessly and emotionlessly (or thoughtlessly) consigned others to the pillory.

THE SHITSTORM MARKET

The increasing squandering of virtuous shitstorms as cyber-bullying could be prevented in a less bloody fashion: with a shitstorm market, similar to Kickstarter. Just as initiators compete to crowdfund their projects there, at a shitstorm market, people could propose shitstorm projects, with the difference being that they would be competing for argumentative and not financial support. The goal would be an objective public discussion of which shitstorm should be carried out, on what grounds, and with what goal. This discussion would end with a vote at a predetermined deadline. If there were a majority—or better, a two-thirds majority—for the proposed shitstorm, it would take place with full momentum.

The shitstorm market would reconcile the discussion model of deliberative democracy with the hunt-and-bait model of the new form of protest. Emotionality and aggression, insults and cruelty would then only be the intentionally uncontrolled implementation of a coolly and fairly discussed plan. The intoxication of the storm would be supported by the preceding tranquility of the discussion. The squaring of the circle: a shitstorm of truly democratic stature.

Societal formations generally manifest themselves in their given ruler: in feudal society, the feudal lord; in capitalist society, those who have capital; and in the information age, computer programmers. The powerful people of the present are not those who know a lot (the term "knowledge society" was dropped for good reason), but rather those who know how to gather, evaluate, and disseminate information. Those who write the algorithms that rule the Internet on the back end of the interface increasingly determine the way our society functions.

The derisive technical term for these people is nerds: brilliant at math; as far as literature goes, they're focused on science fiction, comics, and source code; politically indeterminate; generally unflatteringly clothed, socially inept, and in extreme cases wearing glasses held together with tape. Or at least that was the cliché already presented in the 1984 film *Revenge of the Nerds*, and which is still ruthlessly exploited in successful TV shows like *The Big Bang Theory* and *Silicon Valley.*

As the social biotope of the new heroes of our time, Silicon Valley is just one example of how the lives of nerds have improved. By 1996, the documentary *Triumph of the Nerds*, about the development of the computer industry, had already dropped the categorical limitation that its book version included in 1992: *Accidental Empires: How the Boys of Silicon Valley Make Their Millions, Battle Foreign Competition, and Still Can't Get a Date.* Twenty years later, their triumph is complete. Nerds don't just hold the keys to the future and the billions of tomorrow, they've even written fitness apps for themselves and the world, established their horn-rims as the distinguishing characteristic of hipster culture, and they have, as the title of a 2012 article put it, "The Sexiest Job of the 21st Century."[1]

ENGINEERS

Their triumph certainly didn't come overnight, and it didn't start with the computer. It reaches back to the nineteenth century, when nerds *avant la lettre*—engineers, technicians, and other tinkerers—challenged poets and artists for their central position in society. Examples of architecture and inventions attest to the shift in power: Eiffel's tower, Bell's telephone, Tesla's alternating current. But even the realm of art saw changes in its power structure, such as when painting became technical through the advent of photography. And while in Germany the beginning of the century was characterized by Goethe's and Schiller's classicism, by its end, people were discussing the "natural-scientific basis of poetry."[2]

Once the success could no longer be denied, it was relativized. The German philosopher Ernst Cassirer compared inventors and artists in his 1930 essay "Form and Technology," since both create from themselves, giving their work over to the world full of relief and hope after carrying it within themselves for years. However, while the "work of a discoverer or inventor" belongs to the world from that point on, and must speak for itself in the context of practical use, an artist's work remains tied to her or him and can never be understood without reference to its creator.[3]

What first appears to be an equation turns out to be a degradation, in which cutting the cord is inversely proportional to creativity. A technician, according to Cassirer, is not a real creator, but rather a discoverer: someone who finds something that was already there, but which would have remained concealed without this dis-coverer. That's why discoveries belong to the whole world, independent of the person and personality of their inventor—unlike the creations of artists, which always remain dependent upon them.

But aren't artists also accessories to history, helping things come to light whose time it is—"the antennae of the race," as Ezra Pound put it? And aren't inventors different from discoverers, and isn't the work of the former different from that of the latter? After all, a telephone or computer mouse can be patented, but the law of gravity and Archimedes' principle cannot. Whatever conclusions one comes to, the theory that is advanced in the following text alleges a conspiracy that is based on an enduring slight.

REVENGE

The poets, adventurers, and bon vivants who recite romantic verses, tell crazy stories, and have clever sayings at the ready: they do well everywhere, and they get a pass everywhere. At the pool, for example: they enjoy themselves, lose track of time, show up at the exit twenty minutes after their pass expired, where no doubt a young woman is waiting who likes blue eyes and charming words. As is so often the case, the dawdler passes through without additional payment, and possibly even with a date for that evening! Not so for the nerds. And not because the young woman would act horribly toward them, but because they would be so inhibited toward her. They don't know how to negotiate, and especially not when it's so clear who is in the wrong.

The nerds' nemesis is less the jock than the charmer, the beguiler, the sly dog, the rogue, the rascal, the horse trader, the swindler. Trickery and entrapment, cunning and shrewdness—qualities in which nerds do not invest. In the nerds' ideal world, there are no advantages to having blue eyes and eloquent lips, no *jeitinhos* for *malandros* as they would say in Brazil, no wiggle room between *either* and *or*, 1 and 0. In this world, there are armbands that you hold under a scanner when exiting. The machine punishes those who come too late. In this world, the man doesn't speak to the woman (who was laid off long ago), but rather the armband to the barrier—and it wants additional payment even for two minutes, without looking at the customer, blind to blue eyes and charming smiles, like Lady Justice, and rigid as an algorithm.

The nerds' innate form of communication is the logic of programming: clear if-then directives for everything in life, including the swimming pool. And this is precisely what is happening through the increasing computerization of human interactions. The goal is a society of control in which nothing is up for negotiation and inquiries aren't even possible. In this society, doors open or close based on whether the data fit or not—and if the door sometimes remains closed even if we're sure that we've done everything right, that doesn't necessarily indicate a failure on the part of the nerds; it could also be their revenge. Digital society is a double win for the nerds: first, if there is no communication beyond mathematics, their opponents have been disarmed; second, if everything is programmed, then of course programmers have a home-court advantage—and if even they happen to stay in the water too long, they can hack their way out of the swimming pool if need be.

BREAKING THE LAW

Hacking isn't just the nerds' way of flirting with the woman at the counter; it's also their way of being criminal, from cons and bank robberies to blackmail and sabotage. The magic words of the future are *ransomware* and *malware*, with which computer systems—in cars, companies, hospitals, or nuclear power plants—can be controlled and more or less literally run off a cliff if the ransom isn't paid. The gangster-nerd can get by without a crowbar or a gun, and if there's a chase scene, it happens on the information highway—with the exception of a few culture industry aberrations like Michael Mann's action film *Blackhat* (2015), in which a hacker plays a superhero à la James Bond without ever having appeared as a nerd à la Clark Kent.

The better nerds among the criminals are the cyber-guerillas and Robin Hoods of our time, who liberate data on their own or in "release groups": copy-protected films, games, and programs, or highly explosive secret documents. Martyrs of the "movement"—such as Julian Assange and Edward Snowden, who paid with their freedom—show just how political these acts of liberation can be. At the same time, the hackers' explosive political potential demonstrates itself in these cases, as in spring 2016, when an anonymous person calling themselves John Doe gave the liberated Panama Papers to the *Süddeutsche Zeitung*. They contained eleven million files about the shady dealings of various companies, politicians, and super-wealthy people in Panama. A moment of glory for the nerds as Robin Hoods who help the Fourth Estate, the powerless and the swindled, the humiliated and the insulted of this world to at least get some satisfaction from the rich and powerful. The fictive prototype of this desk-bound Robin Hood is Elliot Alderson in Sam Esmail's TV series *Mr. Robot*: a nerd who doesn't like Steve Jobs or Mark Zuckerberg, socially awkward with a social conscience, who programs for an IT company by day and hacks the computer networks of ruthless corporations by night.

How cool is a John Doe or Edward Snowden, compared to a Kobe Bryant or Justin Bieber! How cool, when Anonymous declares war on ISIS! How pedantic to speak of the nerds' abuse of power when the demand for radical transparency is being dictatorially implemented with no patience for counterarguments.[4] Or does it actually reek of vigilante justice when hackers attack Sony's servers because Sony's lawyers sued release legend George Hotz for hacking Sony's PlayStation 3? Has a lawless space come into existence, where the law of the stronger prevails once again, only now the strength (programming ability) comes not from our muscles but from our brains?

MIDAS'S GOLD

This abuse of power seems nearly innocent when compared with the nerds' pretense to play the role of the hero on both sides of the barricades. They themselves (as programmers or startups) establish the foundations of the system that they undermine (as hackers or crackers). They are the "architects, masons, and maintenance people of the burgeoning digital society."[5] Their triumph has been so radical that they even have dauntless military careers, because in the cyber war, we no longer have to get over the ramparts but through the firewall. And any high-school student who knows how to program social bots—which are now responsible for 20 percent of the activity on Twitter and have a big future on other social networks too—can rise to the level of a demagogue without giving a single speech to the people. As soon as the higher number beats out the better argument, the programmer beats out the intellectual, because every bot strengthens the former's argument.[6]

Wherever nerds conquer new terrain in society, it generally happens by the logic of the computer, so that everything they touch becomes a phenomenon of numbers—with dangerous long-term consequences, similar to those of

King Midas's touch. So friendship becomes a matter of likes, communication becomes a battle for popularity, self-awareness becomes "self-knowledge through numbers" (as the slogan of the Quantified Self movement puts it), dating becomes a matter of compatibility percentages, and erotic adventure becomes a swiping motion of the thumb. And when the introverted nerds have their "coming out" as athletes, it occurs as a "hack" and a "reboot" of their own "operating system," as programmer Bruce Perry explains in his 2012 book *Fitness for Geeks: Real Science, Great Nutrition, and Good Health.* But that isn't all.

For a few years, the "nerds' accession to power in the humanities" has been a locus of fear or hope, depending on which camp you come from.[7] "Digital humanities" is the key phrase, and the fear is that it might suppress anything that could cause worry for data scientists in the humanities: the imprecision of the hermeneutic undertaking. If narration (because what else is interpretation?) yields to numbers (concrete elements in texts or images), thought yields to discovery: driving the human out of the humanities occurs as the "quantitative turn." This turn becomes tangible when job descriptions for literature professorships increasingly include a research focus at the intersection of philology and computer science. Digital lexicography takes the place of ever-new interpretations of a Rilke poem that remains ever the same. A seizure of power can hardly go any better than this.

The change in control has also affected journalism, which was already suffering from the nerds' success because their products took away the journalists' advertising income and audience. The most powerful editor in the world never attended journalism school or took a course in political science; he studied computer science and built a website that reaches more people today than the most important newspapers in the G8 nations taken together. With Facebook, Mark Zuckerberg established a network empire that forces journalism into the cage of Facebook "news," and not just with concepts like "instant articles." At the same time, Zuckerberg subjects public opinion to the logic of programming, which leads to a Facebook ban on anything that violates good taste or political correctness, as Zuckerberg and his algorithms understand it, which includes photos of nursing mothers that show too much breast.

The problematic nature of this shift in power became absurdly evident when one of the icons of engaged journalism—Nick Ut's photo of Vietnamese children fleeing a napalm bombing, with nine-year-old Kim Phúc naked at the center of the image—was banned from Facebook as child pornography. At moments like this, the old public sphere still defends itself copiously, forcing Zuckerberg to retract the erasure of the photo. Anyone who has misgivings about the discussion-free authoritarian way in which Facebook exercises its censorship power doesn't have much to look forward to, once news no longer reaches its audience without Facebook, and the most powerful editor in the world must no longer listen to criticism from some editor-in-chief of a newspaper in Norway or wherever.[8]

It's generally known that algorithms can't read between the lines or distinguish nakedness from pornography. Too much context overwhelms if-then logic. It's less well-known that emoticons were born not out of this interpretive incompetence on the part of the programs, but on the part of the programmers. Back when writing on the Internet was still completely reserved for nerds, it happened again and again that funny comments were accidentally taken seriously. In oral communication, a wink might have cleared the matter up, but writing lacked these finer shades. That's why on September 19, 1982, MIT doctoral student and later computer science professor Scott Elliot Fahlman wrote on a message board at Carnegie Mellon University: "I propose that [*sic*] the following character sequence for joke markers: :-) Read it sideways. Actually, it is probably more economical to mark things that are NOT jokes, given current trends. For this, use :-(."[9]

This was the hour of the emoticon's birth as a series of ASCII characters that, as you can read on Wikipedia, "express a person's feelings or mood." The emoticon—*emot* refers to emotion, *icon* to picture—is the visual depiction of irony. The irony of the story lies in the fact that in 2015— long after emoticons had developed from alphanumeric symbols (periods, commas, dashes, parentheses) into pictograms—an emoji-heir to this joke marker (the "Face with Tears of Joy") was declared Word of the Year by Oxford Dictionaries. Behind this irony is a serious message from the victors: the nerds' method of pointing out irony rather than leaving it to the interpretive skills of communication participants has been accepted worldwide.

Art also hasn't been spared in this shift from new interpretations and conceptions to quantification and visualization; nerds themselves want to portray data analysis as art. Thus, Google has its own data arts team, which proclaims that visualizations of data (the movements of airplanes in US airspace, for example) are art. Other "data artists" create images and sculptures from data about their sleep activity.[10] The results are visually interesting formations whose fascination no doubt grows with their size and level of detail. Thus, statistics are elevated to art by reducing art to decoration. In other words, art takes on the characteristics that Cassirer attributed to technology (revelation of the concealed, discovery instead of creation), supplemented with attractive visual treatments. No wonder such "art" is increasingly discussed in science magazines.

TRIUMPH

On the other hand, isn't technology art precisely because it turns art into technology? Doesn't this paradigm shift in art amount to much more than mere discovery, but rather the creation and (re)formation above all of what art means in twenty-first-century society? It's no coincidence that Steve Jobs's first words in the 1999 docu-fiction film *Pirates of Silicon Valley* aren't about discovery but creation: "We are creating a completely new consciousness, like an artist or a poet." With these pretensions, while trying to lure John Scully away from Pepsi, Jobs asks Scully if he wants to spend the rest of his life selling sugar water, or if he wants to change the world. It was no exaggeration. Jobs truly changed the world. He really did create a completely new consciousness, earning his status as a cult figure by the time of his death.

Jobs was an artist in nerd's clothing who experimented with drugs and had friendships and romances with pop stars. He was more of a designer than an engineer, and he taught the world to feel like a Mac rather than a PC. Jobs is the negation of Bill Gates, as well as of programming genius and Apple cofounder Steve Wozniak, of course. Jobs freed the nerds of their trauma. He preached the aesthetic of fonts and taught non-nerds not to fear technology. Since Jobs, it's been cool to work with computers; thanks to him, computers became a technology that even poets, adventurers, bon vivants, and athletes couldn't forgo—and especially not once it finally fit in the palm of your hand.

That also improved life for nerds who held onto the stereotypical nerd existence. That's because, whereas the world used to be divided into those who played sports and those who sat in front of a computer, now it consists of those who spend their lives at a computer, and those who actually understand them. How absurd would it be to make fun of the latter. And not just because we need them to get the printer to work. Nerds are no longer the IT guys who used to set up WinWord for us. They're the people who determine our culture and tell us the direction it's heading. They've arrived at the point predicted by the TV series *Modern Family* (episode: "After the Fire") in 2011, when intelligent Alex, revered by the nerds at school, explains to her more attractive sister Haley: "You have your fans, I have mine. Someday your fans are going to work for my fans."

Sex, vacation, or job interview—everything we experience can be internally recorded and later viewed again, either alone or with friends, on an external screen. This, at least, is how it was in the episode "The Entire History of You," which aired in December 2011 as part of the British science fiction TV series *Black Mirror*. It was music to the ears of Mark Zuckerberg, who laid out $2 billion to purchase the virtual reality technology Oculus Rift. "We'll have AR [artificial reality] and other devices that we can wear almost all the time to improve our experience and communication. One day, I believe we'll be able to send full, rich thoughts to each other directly using technology. You'll just be able to think of something and your friends will immediately be able to experience it too if you'd like."[1] This is how Zuckerberg, in the summer of 2015, describes Facebook's plans for immersive 360-degree videos. He calls this "the ultimate communication technology." It is a future that is already well underway.

COMMUNICATION WITHOUT A VOICE

That it was possible to document experiences without describing them had already been proclaimed by Zuckerberg at Facebook's Developers Conference in 2011, under the slogan "frictionless sharing." Concretely, what this means is that the song that you are listening to on Spotify and the film you are watching on Netflix, for example, are automatically displayed to your Facebook friends if you have activated the corresponding function. You no longer need to give a reason for this piece of news, or even articulate it. You no longer describe your activities meaningfully, after the fact, as you might once have done using an earlier form of self-representation such as a letter or a diary, and writing something like: "Today, read a book that is on my mind a lot because ..." Now the activities communicate themselves. The new slogan is not "I share therefore I am," but "*It* posts, therefore I am." Because the process lacks a conscious element, it no longer has much to do with Descartes's formula for self-knowledge.

Actually, the muting begins even earlier, while we are still pressing the button ourselves to transmit the photos, spontaneously and unreflectively, that let the network know what we are doing. Since Snapchat has been deleting the photos after they are viewed, we are saying even less about what we are doing or how we feel, and just sending snapshots instead: me in the gym, me after exercising, me in the restaurant, me in front of the window, me in front of the television ... By the end of the evening, committed Snapchatters themselves may hardly know what all they have communicated in this manner over the course of the day. But that doesn't matter either, and this is precisely the point.

The visualization of communication can be conceived as the twenty-first century's technical response to the crisis of representation in the twentieth. The inadequacy of language is cured with nonverbal means. A picture isn't just worth a thousand words—the main thing is that it is no longer necessary to come up with even one. Things communicate themselves when they are photographed or registered automatically. This is why, in 1927, Siegfried Kracauer called photography the "go-for-broke game of history (*Vabanquespiel der Geschichte*)."[2] For one thing, the self-representation of things frees them from human distortion; at the same time, the mechanical reproduction of reality makes our conscious grasp of it superfluous. This role of photography as a means of "organizing a strike against understanding" is where Kracauer saw the historic risk.[3]

AUTOMATIC AUTOBIOGRAPHY

Ninety years later, the stakes have risen. Not only things, but human beings are recording and reproducing themselves, and doing it in ways that bypass the threshold of consciousness. On Facebook and other social networks, we "describe" our life by living it, and in the process we produce an autobiography that has never passed through our brain. Simultaneously, the algorithms are very precisely registering what is happening, as it happens. Zuckerberg's employees are currently working out the details of AI (artificial intelligence) technologies that recognize all the objects in an image and have the capacity to treat them as information. This means that the photos show not only when and where they were made, but what was on the plate in the restaurant and what film was playing on TV. The algorithm can easily extract the corresponding data on nutritional value and cultural capital from the Internet—and consequently knows more about us, thanks to information we transmit, than we do ourselves.

It is this knowledge gap that is the source of the problem. As we give more and more data to the algorithms, we ourselves process less and less of it. The more our speaking, naming, and describing are supplanted by automatic registration and audiovisual copying, the less we ourselves are forced to reflect on and come to terms with the world and our role in it. Language is the medium with which we establish distance from the world, in order to see and understand it more clearly. Every attempt to transcend language also risks the loss of cognition.

For this reason, the BBC slogan "We don't just report a story, we live it" is quite problematic. Above all, it is problematic that Zuckerberg imagines the future of journalism in precisely this way: "more immersive content like VR," more "rich content" instead of "just text and photos." "We're entering this new golden age of video," Zuckerberg told BuzzFeed News in the spring of 2016: "I wouldn't be surprised if you fast-forward five years and most of the content that people see on Facebook and are sharing on a day-to-day basis is video."[4] But what happens, in days to come, if people who witness something on Facebook's video livestream, or via Oculus Rift, won't accept the laborious research of experts? What if, when something occurs, we are no longer compelled to put it into words, but can simply play it on the screen for others? What happens if we are no longer even taking the time to manipulate the images of ourselves that we post, because it isn't possible to do that with live videos?

Kracauer characterized photography as the self-annunciation of material things.[5] Seventy years later, French philosopher Jean Baudrillard would dramatize the process as the "contest between the will of the subject to impose order, a point of view, and the will of the object to impose itself in its discontinuity and momentariness." The winners in this contest are the objects, which give a factual report on "the state of the world in our absence."[6] That this, admittedly, is a win for both sides is suggested by Baudrillard's explanation of the pleasure we feel in taking photographs: "Overall, when it comes to making sense, the world is quite disappointing. Seen in detail and caught by surprise, it is always fully and perfectly evident."[7] We let the objects speak so the void left by our falling mute is filled; the more detail, the better.

In Mark Zuckerberg's communication utopia, the aim is to apply this model to humanity itself: the subject should engage in self-display, bypassing consciousness. When Zuckerberg talks about the video trend he has identified, he stresses that he is not talking about films whose content or form have been intentionally shaped; he is talking about the coveted "raw material" of social life. The paradoxical result is an automatic autobiography that we "write" *by living*—a posthuman, algorithmic autobiography.

SELFIE SOCIETY WITHOUT SELF-CONSCIOUSNESS

Facebook's mission is emblazoned on its welcome page: "Connect with friends and the world around you on Facebook." This culture of connecting and communicating guarantees that Facebook users remain surrounded by "friends" from earlier periods of their lives and many other people they scarcely know—not only across geographical or biographical boundaries, but also regardless of ideological differences.

The official goal of this culture is to contribute to world peace. Truly, Facebook's chief operating officer Sheryl Sandberg was reaching for these heights when she posed the rhetorical question: "But is it harder to shoot at someone who you've connected to personally? Yeah. Is it harder to hate when you've seen pictures of that person's kids? We think the answer is yes."[8] Later, Zuckerberg delivered a version of the same viewpoint in the context of a UN meeting at which he argued for access to the Internet as a universal human right: "A 'like' or a post won't stop a tank or a bullet, but when people are connected, we have a chance to build a common global community with a shared understanding."[9]

The irony—and hidden precondition—of this global understanding is that people have to stop understanding themselves. Precondition, because the old problem of identity construction is the boundary that—for individuals as well as nations—usually accompanies it and initially works against unification. The dominance of subjects over objects consists fundamentally in the development of a specific individual perspective, which, as such, is in opposition to the specific perspective of another individual. Distance is created by taking a position on things, not by merging with them. The hope for a world community lies in immersing the ego in the world that surrounds it, in a self that, no matter how many selfies it posts, is not overly conscious of itself.

What is easier than criticizing Facebook? It takes gossip for friendship, voyeurism for solidarity, and trivia for information. It has industrialized sharing and generates huge revenues from it. It is a permanent assessment center and an incredible waste of time. Yes, sure, of course. But, don't people see the real benefit of Facebook? Don't they realize how effectively it answers a basic social problem in a technical way? Does nobody remember the famous saying by Blaise Pascal? Or at least the popular song by John Lennon?

It was 1974 when Lennon's "Whatever Gets You Thru the Night" became a number one hit on the US charts. The most important words in this song are "it's alright." This blank absolution is repeated with increasing emphasis: "Whatever Gets You Thru Your Life," "Whatever Gets You to the Light": "It's alright, alright." It remains unclear what the recurring "whatever" stands for, but we know where Lennon picked up the line: from a popular African-American evangelist during late night TV channel surfing. Obviously Lennon hit a nerve. He sang away an old existential problem—the horror vacui—in joyful rhythms. How so?

THE HORROR OF QUIET CHAMBERS

About three hundred years earlier the French philosopher Blaise Pascal wrote: "All the unhappiness of men arises from one single fact, that they cannot stay quietly in their own chamber." Alone, Pascal believes, everybody "feels his nothingness, his forlornness, his insufficiency, his dependence, his weakness, his emptiness." His being prone to death haunts every human, "so that if he be without what is called diversion, he is unhappy."[1] Which is why one doesn't want to be given the hare one is hunting. As Pascal says: "The hare in itself would not screen us from the sight of death and calamities; but the chase which turns away our attention from these, does screen us."

More important than killing the hare is killing time. A century after Pascal, the quiet chamber problem was solved: the book invited distraction into any empty room, the lamp even after dark, with television one made it through the night even without additional light.

And through life. Because getting through was more and more the issue in the twentieth century. Pascal, it should be said, referred his readers to God. In God, being is meaning, the holy scripture replaces the fear of silence by the feeling of security. But what if God is dead, as Nietzsche announced at the end of the nineteenth century? How could we live after the end of philosophical and political narratives announced by Lyotard and after the fall of the socialist systems? And what of the end of utopia, optimism, history? There are three options: one accepts hopelessness, reanimates God, or looks for another narcotic that gets one through the night and life.

NARCOTICS

Let's start with accepting hopelessness. It was in 1985 that the Italian philosopher Gianni Vattimo said that after the end of grand narratives that gave meaning to life and history, philosophers are no longer expected to show people where they are going but instead how to live with the condition of not going anywhere.[2] That same year the rock band Talking Heads translated this philosophical insight into defiant fatalism: "We're on a road to nowhere / Come on inside."

Second, the reanimation of God: When Nietzsche said: "We have killed God" he also asked: Isn't this murder too big for us? Don't we now have to become gods ourselves? And indeed, it was too much—and the twentieth century ended with the return of religion—although in spiritual rather than confessional form.

The third response to the metaphysical void of modernity was television, the most effective narcotic of the second half of the twentieth century, particularly since the rise of private cable channels that didn't comply with any educational mandate and aimed at sheer distraction. The results are reported in a famous essay by the German poet and intellectual Hans-Magnus Enzensberger in 1988 with the provocative title: "Absolute Emptiness: The Null-Medium, or Why All Complaints about Television Are Irrelevant." Enzensberger's emptiness is the opposite of Pascal's quietness. It is a hypnotic immersion into the flashy cycle of images devoid of any messages. Enzensberger's main witness is a six-month-old baby in front of the screen. The baby is not yet cognitively capable of understanding—but nevertheless sits magnetized and happy; a symbol of an intensive moment liberated from any meaning.

Many will be able to subscribe to Enzensberger's model. However, if you think about it, the baby is not really a good example since the author overestimates the appeal of non-sense to those whose cognitive skills are more developed. To adults, distraction without the alibi of meaning would not conceal the human dilemma but underline it. Therefore, adults need a story between the flashy images no matter how hollow, incoherent, or interchangeable. This, at least, is how it has worked thus far. Nowadays we need stronger measures.

DISTRACTION 2.0

For digital natives, perfect distraction lies in permanent communication combined with interaction. It needs other people. This has led some observers to consider Facebook as the fitting technology for neuroscientific theories of empathy. Some have even celebrated Facebook as a medium of love, as a utopia of communication beyond the principles of hierarchical and utilitarian thinking. Such a defense of Facebook against its shortsighted critics is brave but still misleading. It entertains the illusion that humans are on the road to a better world.

Let's assume the following: interaction on social networks is more or less what in linguistics is called phatic communication and in common parlance small talk. A kind of placebo conversation referring to nothing but itself and the immediate moment. More precisely, the aim is to avoid the moment that, like Pascal's quiet chamber, would leave one alone with oneself. Permanent communication has become the ruling principle of contemporary culture. Sometimes, it may feel like a burden. But in moments when life forces idleness upon us (in the waiting room, on the bus) we feel the fear of death once more and rush to our smartphones. New media guarantee that you will never be alone with yourself. Their promise: to keep you busy, to take care of your downtime. No room for horror vacui.

Remember Pascal's hare hunting? In the twenty-first century it takes place on Facebook, and Twitter, and mobile media. The alternative to God is new media; the priest is replaced by the programmer. The project of modernity—which would otherwise be challenged by a return to God—can continue by way of the turn to technology. Technology translates religion—from *ligare*: to bind, connect—as link and makes online networks, rather than the pulpit, the medium of salvation.

FACEBOOK'S WHATEVER

On online networks, social encounters occur with the frequency and speed of the "update," celebrating an eternal recurrence of the same. The philosophical punch line of this translation: as long as they keep the carousel of communication alive, Facebook users cannot escape a Weltanschauung of cheerfulness. It is the metaphysics of aimlessness; the bliss of every communication junkie.

Against all the talk about the capitalization of private data and the evil of Facebook, one needs to see the bigger picture. It is time to understand the enormous opportunity Facebook is giving humankind. It is time to acknowledge that Zuckerberg's invention has made the social not only measurable but also sustainable. It is taking care of the problem of meaning in life by getting rid of any time to wonder. Whatever the "Whatever" was in Lennon's famous song, these days we know: it's Facebook.[3]

Notes

WASTE: AN INTRODUCTION

1. The German term *Abfall*, the title of this book, has an array of meanings. It can refer to a by-product or waste, but it can also denote a separation: dissent, secession, a break with something. It often describes something incidental or contrary to a central entity.—Trans.

2. Pressestelle des Bundesgerichtshofs, press release no. 14/13, Jan. 24, 2013, http://juris.bundesgerichtshof.de/cgi -bin/rechtsprechung/document.py?Gericht=bgh&Art=pm &pm_nummer=0014/13.

3. Ruchika Agarwal, "Here Is Why We Should Thank Microsoft for Its AI Bot That Turned into a Foul-Mouthed Racist," *Business Insider*, March 30, 2016, http://www.businessinsider. com/why-microsofts-chatbot-tay-should-make-us-look -at-ourselves; Julie Bort, "Google Shocked This Man by Offering Sympathy on the Death of His Father," *Business Insider*, March 31, 2016, http://www.businessinsider.com/google -now-offers-a-man-condolences-2016-3.

4. "Smile, You're on BinCam! Five Households Agree to Let Snooping Device Record Everything They Throw Away," *Daily Mail*, http://www.dailymail.co.uk/news/article-2000566/ Smile-Youre-bin-cam-The-snooping-device-record-throw -away.html, March 4, 2011.

5. Hans Blumenberg, *Theorie der Unbegrifflichkeit* (*Theory of Non-Conceptuality*) (Frankfurt: Suhrkamp, 2007), 9.

6. Blumenberg, *Theorie*, 11–12. "It [the concept] must possess enough clarity to differentiate that which is absolutely not

pertinent, but its exclusivity should not be as narrow as a name for identifying an individual and their identity" (12).

7. Hans Blumenberg, *Paradigms for a Metaphorology*, translated by Robert Savage (1997; Ithaca: Cornell University Press, 2010), 3; previous quotation: Hans Blumenberg, "Prospect for a Theory of Non-Conceptuality," in *Shipwreck with Spectator*, translated by Steven Rendall (1979; Cambridge, MA: MIT Press, 1997), 81.

8. For the courage of the mind to conjecture, see Blumenberg, *Paradigms for a Metaphorology*, 5. Blumenberg justifies his shift in perspective (three years after Paul Feyerabend's anarchistic theory of scientific inquiry in *Against Method*) from the conceptual to the lifeworld (as the constant "motivating support ... of all theory") with fundamental doubt of knowledge: "Although we must already understand that we cannot expect *the truth* from science, we would like at least to know why we wanted to know what we now find ourselves disappointed knowing. In this sense, metaphors are fossils that indicate an archaic stratum of the trial of theoretical curiosity." Blumenberg. "Prospect for a Theory of Non-Conceptuality," 81–82; Andreas Huyssen, *Miniature Metropolis: Literature in an Age of Photography and Film* (Cambridge, MA: Harvard University Press, 2015).

9. Theodor W. Adorno, "The Essay as Form," translated by Bob Hullot-Kentor and Frederic Will, *New German Critique*, no. 32 (Spring—Summer, 1984): 151–171, 160. For a critique of the escape into the metaphorical as well as into dialectical incantation at the cost of making a clear statement of one's own "quite speculative theory," see Adorno's letter to Walter Benjamin from November 10, 1938. The latter answers this accusation of "missing theoretical transparency" in his letter to Adorno from December 9, 1938. *The Correspondence of Walter Benjamin, 1910–1940*, edited by Gershom Scholem et al. (Chicago: University of Chicago Press, 1994), 582, 598.

10. Adorno, "The Essay as Form," 157, 159.

11. Adorno, "The Essay as Form," 161, 161, 165, 166, 166.

12. Adorno, "The Essay as Form," 152, 156. See also Michel Foucault, "The Order of Discourse," in *Untying the Text: A Post-Structuralist Reader*, edited by Robert Young (Boston: Routledge, 1981), 51–78.

13. Adorno, "The Essay as Form," 166; quote from Max Bense, "Über den Essay und seine Prosa" [On the essay and its prose], *Merkur* 1 (1947): 420.

14. Adorno, "The Essay as Form," 166.

15. Adorno, "The Essay as Form," 164; quote from Max Bense, "Über den Essay und seine Prosa," 418.

CHAPTER 1

1. Mark Weinstein, "Did Facebook Really Elect Trump President?" *Huffington Post*, Nov. 25, 2016, https://www.huffingtonpost.com/mark-weinstein/did-facebook-really-elect_b_13208968.html; "US Election 2016: Trump's 'Hidden' Facebook Army," BBC, Nov. 15, 2016, http://www.bbc.com/news/blogs-trending-37945486; Jonas Jansen, "Hass im Internet: Ermittlungen gegen Facebook-Chef Zuckerberg" [Hate on the Internet: Investigation into Facebook-founder Zuckerberg], *Süddeutsche Zeitung*, Nov. 4, 2016, http://www.faz.net/aktuell/wirtschaft/netzwirtschaft/hass-im-internet-ermittlungen-gegen-facebookchef-zuckerberg-14512780.html; Bernhard Pörksen, "Die Schuldfrage" [The guilt question], *Die Zeit*, Nov. 11, 2016, http://www.zeit.de/kultur/2016-11/medien-us-wahl-donald-trump-schuld; Rich McCormick, "Donald Trump Says Facebook and Twitter 'Helped Him Win,'" *The Verge*, Nov. 13, 2016, https://www.theverge.com/2016/11/13/13619148/trump-facebook-twitterhelped-win; Dan Tynan, "How Facebook Powers Money Machines for Obscure Political 'News' Sites," *Guardian*, Aug. 24, 2016, https://www.theguardian.com/technology/2016/aug/24/facebook-clickbait-political-news-sites-us-election-trump.

2. Leon Festinger, *Theory of Cognitive Dissonance* (Stanford: Stanford University Press, 1957); Andrew Shapiro, *The Control Revolution: How the Internet Is Putting Individuals in Charge and Changing the World We Know* (New York: PublicAffairs, 1999).

3. Mark Zuckerberg, Facebook post on Nov. 13, 2016, http://www.facebook.com/zuck/posts/10103253901916271.

4. Mark Zuckerberg's Facebook page on Nov. 9, 2016, at 8 p.m.: "I thought about all the work ahead of us to create the world we want for our children. This work is bigger than any presidency and progress does not move in a straight line."

CHAPTER 2

1. Johann Wolfgang von Goethe, *Faust: A Tragedy, Part One*, translated by Martin Greenburg (New Haven, CT: Yale University Press, 1992), 53.

2. Thomas Hylland Eriksen, *Tyranny of the Moment: Fast and Slow Time in the Information Age* (London: Pluto Press, 2001); Douglas Rushkoff, *Present Shock: When Everything Happens Now* (New York: Penguin, 2013).

3. On May 29, 2016, at a concert in Verona, British singer Adele said to a female fan "Could you stop filming me with that video camera? Because I'm really here in real life, you can enjoy it in real life rather than through your camera." "Adele Tells Fan to Stop Filming Gig and Enjoy It in Real Life," *Guardian*, May 31, 2016, https://www.theguardian.com/music/2016/may/31/adele-tells-fan-to-stop-filming-gig-and-enjoy-it-in-real-life.

4. Christopher Lasch, *The Culture of Narcissism: American Life in an Age of Diminishing Expectations* (New York: W. W. Norton, 1991), 12 ("imperial self," "narcissistic, infantile, empty self"), 13 ("psychological man," "mental health").

CHAPTER 3

1. Stefan Krempl, "Bundestag beschließt 'Zwangsbeglückung' mit intelligenten Stromzählern" [Bundestag approves "obligatory improvement": Smart electricity meters], *heise online*, June 26, 2016, https://www.heise.de/newsticker/meldung/Bundestag -beschliesst-Zwangsbeglueckung-mit-intelligenten-Strom zaehlern-3248056.html.

CHAPTER 4

1. "Nam June Paik—Good Morning Mr. Orwell (1984)," YouTube video, 57:56, posted by mysteriuminiquitatis, Nov. 20, 2013, https://www.youtube.com/watch?v=SlQLhyDljtl (accessed Feb. 4, 2018), Plimpton quotation, 5:45–6:20, Sapho quotation, 8:12.

2. Wikipedia, "Big Brother Awards," https://de.wikipedia.org/ wiki/Big_Brother_Awards (accessed Jan. 10, 2018).

3. "Motorola Xoom 'Empower the People'—Super Bowl Commercial 2011," YouTube video, 1:00, posted by Mobilegeeks. de, Feb. 6, 2011, https://www.youtube.com/watch?v=gwBN69 -esPs (accessed Jan. 18, 2018).

4. "Sergey Brin and Larry Page: Inside the Google Brother's Master Mission," YouTube video, 23:35 (at 19:55ff), posted by Bloomberg, June 3, 2014, https://www.youtube.com/watch ?v=gtMkq6IxVKk (accessed Jan. 18, 2018).

5. Derek Thompson, "Google's CEO: 'The Laws Are Written by Lobbyists,'" *Atlantic*, Oct. 1, 2010, http://www.theatlantic .com/technology/archive/2010/10/googles-ceo-the-laws -are-written-by-lobbyists/63908.

6. The term "consciousness industry" (*Bewusstseinsindustrie*) was coined by Hans Magnus Enzensberger in his 1964 essay of the same title, in *Einzelheiten* (Frankfurt: Suhrkamp, 1982).—Trans.

7. Max Horkheimer and Theodor W. Adorno, *Dialectic of Enlightenment*, translated by J. Cumming (New York: Continuum, 1991), 14. Translation modified.

8. Nick Bilton, "Steve Jobs Was a Low-Tech Parent," *New York Times*, Sept. 10, 2014, https://www.nytimes.com/2014/09/11/fashion/steve-jobs-apple-was-a-low-tech-parent.html.

CHAPTER 5

1. Immanuel Kant, "Idea for a Universal History with a Cosmopolitan Purpose," in *Kant: Political Writings*, 2nd ed., edited by Hans Reiss, translated by H. B. Nisbet (1784; Cambridge: Cambridge University Press, 1991), 41–53, at 42.

2. Johann Gottfried Herder, *Herders Sämmtliche Werke* [Herder's complete works], vol. 14, edited by Bernhard Suphan (Berlin: Weidmann, 1909), 236.

3. Quoted in Reinhart Koselleck and Horst Günther, "Geschichte" [History], in *Geschichtliche Grundbegriffe: Historisches Lexikon zur politisch-sozialen Sprache in Deutschland* [Fundamental historical concepts: Historical dictionary of political-social language in Germany], vol. 2, edited by Otto Brunner, Werner Conze, und Reinhart Koselleck (Stuttgart: Klett-Cotta, 1975), 593–717, at 663.

4. Pierre Nora, "Between Memory and History: Les Lieux de Mémoire," *Representations*, no. 26, special issue: "Memory and Counter-Memory" (Spring 1989): 7–24, at 13.

CHAPTER 7

1. Roland Barthes, "Wirklichkeits—oder vielmehr Realitätseffekt (Lacan)" [Verisimilitude, or rather the effect of reality (Lacan)], in *Texte zur Theorie der Fotografie* [Texts on the theory of photography], edited by Bernd Stiegler (Stuttgart: Reclam, 2010), 95–101, at 95, 99.

2. Crispin Startwell, *End of Story: Toward an Annihilation of Language and History* (New York: SUNY Press, 2000), 17.

3. Barthes, "Wirklichkeits," 96, 99; following quotation, 99.

4. Siegfried Kracauer, "Photography," translated by Thomas Y. Levin, *Critical Inquiry* 19, no. 3 (Spring 1993): 421–436, at 427.

5. Kracauer, "Photography," 432 (both quotes).

6. Kracauer, "Photography," 432, 433.

CHAPTER 8

1. Franz Kafka, quoted in Roland Barthes, *Camera Lucida,* translated by Richard Howard (New York: Hill and Wang, 1982), 53.

2. Giorgio Agamben, *Infancy and History: The Destruction of Experience,* translated by Liz Heron (London: Verso, 1993), 15.

3. Michael David Murphy, *Unphotographable,* http://www.unphotographable.com/archives/2008/06/nun.shtml, June 2008; http://www.unphotographable.com/archives/2007/02/pitbull_swingse.shtml, Feb. 2007; http://www.unphotographable.com/archives/2007/06/shopping_and_cr.shtml, June 2007 (accessed Dec. 24, 2017).

CHAPTER 9

1. Bertolt Brecht, "The Radio as an Apparatus of Communication," in *Brecht on Film and Radio,* edited and translated by Mark Silberman (London: Bloomsbury, 2000), 41–48, at 41, 43.

2. Perry Barlow, "Declaration of the Independence of Cyberspace," Electronic Frontier Foundation, Feb. 8, 1996, https://www.eff.org/cyberspace-independence (accessed Jan. 18, 2018).

3. Jürgen Habermas, "Political Communication in Media Society: Does Democracy Still Have an Epistemic Dimension? The Impact of Normative Theory on Empirical Research," chapter 9 in Habermas, *Europe: The Faltering Project,* translated by Ciaran Cronin (Cambridge, MA: Polity Press, 2009), 138.

4. Brecht, "Radio as an Apparatus," 43.

5. Brecht, "Radio as an Apparatus," 43.

6. Frank Koughan and Douglas Rushkoff, *Generation Like*, PBS documentary, 2014, https://www.pbs.org/wgbh/frontline/film/generation-like (accessed Jan. 18, 2018).

7. Mark Zuckerberg, Facebook post on 30 June 2015, http://www.facebook.com/zuck/posts/10102213601037571 (accessed Jan. 18, 2018). The passage that is quoted was in response to a question from Jeff Jarvis; the following quote was in answer to a question from Arianna Huffington.

8. David Kirkpatrick, *The Facebook Effect: The Inside Story of the Company That Is Connecting the World* (New York: Simon and Schuster, 2010), 181.

9. Kirkpatrick, *Facebook Effect*, 181.

CHAPTER 10

1. Pierre Lévy, *Cyberculture*, translated by Robert Bononno (1997; Minneapolis: University of Minnesota Press, 2001), 92.

2. James Surowiecki tells this anecdote at the beginning of his book *The Wisdom of Crowds* (New York: Doubleday, 2005), xi–xii.

3. Eli Pariser, *The Filter Bubble: What the Internet Is Hiding from Us* (New York: Viking, 2011), 14–15. On the stupidity of the crowd, see Surowiecki, *Wisdom of Crowds*.

4. Ellen Gamerman, "When the Art Is Watching You," *Wall Street Journal*, Dec. 11, 2014, https://www.wsj.com/articles/when-the-art-is-watchingyou-1418338759.

5. Rainer Maria Rilke, "Archaic Torso of Apollo" (1908), in *Ahead of All Parting: Selected Poetry and Prose of Rainer Maria Rilke*, translated by Stephen Mitchell (New York: Modern Library, 1995), 67.

6. Manfred Schneider, *Transparenztraum: Literatur, Politik, Medien und das Unmögliche* [Dream of transparency: Literature, politics, media, and the impossible] (Berlin: Matthes & Seitz, 2013). On loss of privacy and the avant-garde of the Internet, see Roberto Simanowski, *Digitale Medien in der Erlebnisgesellschaft: Kultur—Kunst—Utopie* [Digital media in experience-oriented society: culture—art—utopia] (Reinbek bei Hamburg: Rowohlt, 2008), 55–61. On the propagation and practice of the "death of the artist" in the aesthetic of interactive art, see Roberto Simanowski, *Digital Art and Meaning: Reading Kinetic Poetry, Text Machines, Mapping Art, and Interactive Installations* (Minneapolis: University of Minnesota Press, 2011), 53–57, 90–119.

7. Grant H. Kester, *Conversation Pieces: Community and Communication in Modern Art* (Berkeley: University of California Press, 2004); for a critique of this position, see Claire Bishop, *Artificial Hells: Participatory Art and the Politics of Spectatorship* (London: Verso, 2012), 25, with regard to Kester's praise for "compassionate identification with the other" in "participatory art."

CHAPTER 11

1. *Anglizismus des Jahres*, http://www.anglizismusdesjahres .de/anglizismen-des-jahres/adj-2011/ (accessed Dec. 24, 2017).

2. Corinna Justus, July 25, 2012, comment on Facebook, http:// www.facebook.com/vodafoneDE/posts/10150952976257 724 (accessed Dec. 24, 2017).

3. "Hunde lebendig verbrannt für Fussball Em 2012 Ukraine Maja von Hohenzollern ARD Brisant" [Dogs burned alive for soccer championship 2012 Ukraine Maja von Hohenzollern ARD Brisant], YouTube video, 3:40. Posted by TheKingLouis14, Nov. 4, 2011, https://www.youtube.com/watch?v =gwBN69-esPs (accessed Dec. 24, 2017).

4. In 1973, the USSR national soccer team did not attend the second-leg qualifying match for the 1974 World Cup. It was held on the "bloody sod" of the Estadio Nacional in Santiago de Chile, where, following the coup by Augusto Pinochet, approximately 40,000 supporters of the socialist president Salvador Allende had recently been imprisoned and mal-treated, and many were killed. See "Chile gegen UdSSR: Eine geisterhafte Begegnung im Estadio Nacional" [Chile vs. USSR: A ghostly encounter at the Estadio Nacional], *Che Futbol*, Nov. 12, 2017, http://www.chefutbol.com/fur-die-ewigkeit/spiele-fur-die-ewigkeit/chile-gegen-udssr-eine-geisterhafte-begegnung-im-estadio-nacional (accessed Jan. 26, 2018).

5. Tapio Liller, "Tierschützer machen mobil gegen EM-Sponsoren—eine Analyse" [Animal rights activists mobilize against soccer championship sponsors—an analysis], *t3n*, Nov. 25, 2011, http://t3n.de/news/tierschutzer-mobil-gegenem-sponsoren-analyse-346053.

6. Oliver Links, "Im Auge des Shit-Stürmchens" [In the face of the shitstorm], *Brand Eins*, Feb. 2012, 94–99, at 98.

7. Liller, "Tierschützer machen mobil gegen EM-Sponsoren."

8. Stephan Dörner, "Adidas hat ärger im Netz" [Adidas's trouble online], *Handelsblatt*, Nov. 22, 2011; Inga Catharina Thomas, "Tierschützer bezichtigen Ukraine der Lüge" [Animal rights activists accuse Ukraine of lying], *Fokus*, Nov. 25, 2011.

9. Colin Crouch, *Post-Democracy* (Cambridge: Polity, 2004), 111.

10. Lucretius, *De Rerum natura* (*On the Nature of Things*), Book 2, cited in Hans Blumenberg, *Shipwreck with Spectator* (Cambridge, MA: MIT Press, 1996), 114.

11. Johann Osel, "Professoren fürchten den Shitstorm" [Professors fear shitstorms], *Süddeutsche Zeitung*, Jan. 7, 2016, http://www.sueddeutsche.de/bildung/universitaeten-stoersaal-1.2806877 7; Michael Schudson, *The Good Citizen: A History of American Public Life* (New York: The Free Press, 1998).

12. Daria Suharchuk, "Propaganda aus der Trollfabrik" [Propaganda from the troll factory], *Zeit Online*, July 9, 2015, http://www.zeit.de/politik/ausland/2015-07/russland-trolle-enthuellung.

CHAPTER 12

1. Thomas H. Davenport and D. J. Patil, "Data Scientist: The Sexiest Job of the 21st Century," *Harvard Business Review*, Oct. 2012, https://hbr.org/2012/10/data-scientist-the-sexiest-job-of-the-21st-century/ar/1.

2. Wilhelm Bölsche, *Die naturwissenschaftlichen Grundlagen der Poesie: Prolegomena einer realistischen Ästhetik* [The natural-scientific foundations of poetry: Prolegomena to a realistic aesthetic], edited by Johannes J. Braakenburg (1887; Tübingen: Max Niemeyer, 1976).

3. Ernst Cassirer, "Form and Technology," in *Ernst Cassirer on Form and Technology: Contemporary Readings*, edited by Aud Sissel Hoel and Ingvild Folkvord (New York: Palgrave Macmillan, 2012), 15–53, at 46.

4. Jaron Lanier, "The Hazard of Nerd Supremacy: The Case of WikiLeaks," *Atlantic*, Aug. 10, 2011.

5. Sascha Lobo, "Das Nerd-Dilemma" [The nerd dilemma], *Spiegel-Online*, April 10, 2012, http://www.spiegel.de/netzwelt/web/sascha-lobos-kolumne-zu-piratenparteiund-internet-nerds-a-826515.html.

6. Martin Fuchs, "Automatisierte Trolle: Warum Social Bots unsere Demokratie gefährden" [Automated trolls: Why social bots jeopardize our democracy], *Neue Züricher Zeitung*, Sept. 12, 2016, https://www.nzz.ch/digital/automatisierte-trolle-warumsocial-bots-unsere-demokratie-gefaehrden-ld.116166. Among other things, Fuchs reports on the eighteen-year-old Amsterdam high-school student Lennart V., who is paid to program chatbots that believably support certain political positions on the Internet.

7. Thomas Thiel, "Meint der jüngste Aufschwung der Digital Humanities den Machtantritt des Nerds in den Geisteswissenschaften?" [Does the recent digital humanities boom mean nerds are taking control of the liberal arts?], *Frankfurter Allgemeine Zeitung*, July 24, 2012.

8. Anna-Lena Roth, "Chefredakteur kritisiert Facebook-Chef 'Hör zu, Mark, das ist ernst ...'" [editor in chief criticizes Facebook head: "Listen, Mark, this is serious ..."], *Spiegel Online*, Sept. 9, 2016, http://www.spiegel.de/netzwelt/netzpolitik/facebookaftenposten-chef-espen-egil-hansen-kritisiert mark-zuckerberg-per-brief-a-1111551.html. For further information on interventions by Facebook administrators, see Johannes Boie, "Zensur in sozialen Medien: Wie Facebook Menschen zum Schweigen bringt" [Censorship on social media: How Facebook silences people], *Süddeutsche Zeitung*, Aug. 22, 2016, http://www.sueddeutsche.de/digital/zensur-in-sozialen-medien-wie-facebook-menschen-zum -schweigenbringt-1.3130204. Following the public protest against the deletion of the Vietnam War photo (by an employee), Facebook allowed it to be posted on the platform again.

9. Wikipedia contributors, "Emoticon," Wikipedia, https://en .wikipedia.org/w/index.php?title=Emoticon&oldid =818853009 (accessed Jan. 10, 2018).

10. Aaron Koblin, "Data Visions," *Think with Google*, April 2012, https://www.thinkwithgoogle.com/articles/data-visions .html; "Laurie Frick: Data Artist," YouTube video, 21:04, posted by CreativeMornings HQ, April 5, 2014, https://www.youtube .com/watch?v=DXtSXYIHjcg (accessed Jan. 10, 2018).

CHAPTER 13

1. Mark Zuckerberg, quoted in William David, "Mark Zuckerberg and the End of Language," *Atlantic*, Sept. 11, 2015, http://www.theatlantic.com/technology/archive/2015/09/silicon -valley-telepathy-wearables/404641.

2. Siegfried Kracauer, "Photography," translated by Thomas Y. Levin, *Critical Inquiry* 19, no. 3 (Spring 1993): 421–436, at 435.

3. Kracauer, "Photography," 432.

4. Mat Honan, "Why Facebook and Mark Zuckerberg Went All in on Live Video," BuzzFeed, April 6, 2016, https://www.buzz feed.com/mathonan/why-facebook-and-mark-zuckerberg -went-all-in-on-live-video (accessed Jan. 18, 2018).

5. "For in the artwork the meaning of the object takes on spatial appearance, whereas in photography the spatial appearance of an object is its meaning." Kracauer, "Photography," 427.

6. Jean Baudrillard, *Radical Alterity*, translated by Marc Guil-laume (Los Angeles: Semiotext[e], 2008), 149, 152.

7. Jean Baudrillard, *Fotografien 1985–1998*, exhibition catalog, edited by Peter Weibel (Ostfildern-Ruit: Hatje Cantz, 1999), 147.

8. Dan Fletcher, "How Facebook Is Redefining Privacy," *Time*, May 20, 2010, http://content.time.com/time/magazine/ article/0,9171,1990798,00.html (accessed Jan. 18, 2018).

9. "Mark Zuckerberg, Bill Gates Call for Universal Internet Access at UN Summit," *Indian Express*, Sept. 27, 2015, http:// indianexpress.com/article/technology/tech-news-technol ogy/mark-zuckerberg-calls-for-universal-internet-access -at-un-summit (accessed Jan. 18, 2018).

CHAPTER 14

1. Blaise Pascal, *Pascal's Pensées*, translated by W. F. Trotter (New York: Dutton, 1958), no. 139.

2. Gianni Vattimo, *Jenseits vom Subjekt: Nietzsche, Heidegger und die Hermeneutik* [Beyond the subject: Nietzsche, Heidegger, and Hermeneutics] translated by Sonja Puntscher Riek-mann (Vienna: Passagen, 1986), 17.

3. The degree to which Facebook can actually be viewed as the practice of a cosmopolitan community based not on shared values, for example, but on the need to disclose information is an issue I investigate, following on Jean-Luc Nancy's concept of the community, in my book *Facebook Society: Losing Ourselves in Sharing Ourselves* (New York: Columbia University Press, 2018).